ARCHAEOLOGY

The Comic

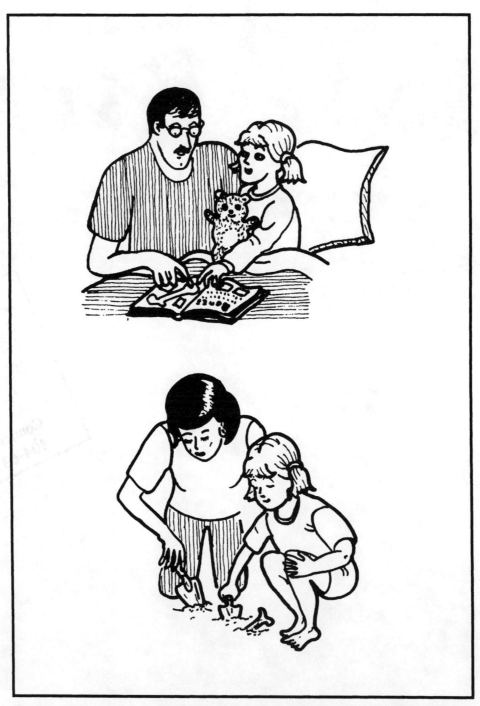

Squizee (skwizee) has always had a sense of wonder for things she finds in books or in the ground. Join her as she learns about the strange world of archaeology and archaeologists . . .

ARCHAEOLOGY

The Comic

Johannes H. N. Loubser

ALTAMIRA
PRESS

A Division of Rowman & Littlefield Publishers, Inc.

Walnut Creek   •   Lanham   •   New York   •   Oxford

ALTAMIRA PRESS
A Division of Rowman & Littlefield Publishers, Inc.
1630 North Main Street #367
Walnut Creek, California 94596
www.altamirapress.com

Rowman & Littlefield Publishers, Inc.
A Member of the Rowman & Littlefield Publishing Group
4720 Boston Way
Lanham, MD 20706

P.O. Box 317
Oxford
OX2 9RU, UK

British Cataloging in Publication Information available

Library of Congress Cataloging-in-Publication Data
Loubser, J. H. N. (Johannes Henoch Neethling)
Archaeology : the comic / Johannes H. N. Loubser.
    p. cm.
  Includes bibliographical references and index.
  ISBN: 0-7591-0380-1 (alk. paper)—0-7591-0381-X (pbk. : alk. paper)
    1. Archaeology—Methodology—Pictorial works. 2. Archaeology—Field
work—Pictorial works. 3. Excavations (Archaeology)—Pictorial works. I. Title.

CC75.7 .L68 2002
741.5'973—dc21

                                                            2002028043

Printed in the United States of America

CONTENTS

*This comic book is dedicated to Susan
Janet, Deborah Ruth, and Sarah Leah*

ACKNOWLEDGMENTS

My new life in the United States of America seemed too good to be true. As a native South African who emigrated to the United States at the end of 1993, I was not used to being given such wonderful opportunities; in the much smaller world of South African publication even accomplished illustrators and storytellers have difficulty getting their works accepted. I thank Mitch Allen of AltaMira Press for his positive attitude and insistence that a comic textbook on archaeology should be published and that I was the person to do it. All I had to do before signing the contract with AltaMira was to show Mitch the first chapter and general outline of the book at the 1996 Society of American Archaeology meeting in New Orleans.

The drawing of the comic has been low-tech and painstaking, taking place mostly in the secluded underworld dungeon below my house. First I copied and drew the cells with a mechanical pencil on Mylar that has blue-line blocks. As my inspiration I used any pictures I could lay my hands on, ranging from Tintin comic books by the extremely talented Belgian cartoonist Hergé to clip-art on the web. The completed pencil drawings with written text served as a draft version of the comic, photocopies of which I mailed for review. The final draft was redrawn in black ink on Mylar. Pattie Rechtman expertly edited and typeset the final product, with the invaluable help of proofreader Nancy Knight. Rachel Rechtman helped design the chapter openings.

As I think I demonstrate in the pages that follow, archaeology is a group effort. The development of this book is no different. I thank dating specialists Allan Watchman (Australia), Balt Verhagen (South Africa), and Marvin Rowe (U.S.A.) for introducing me to the basics of the physical analyses and dating of archaeological materials. Lisa O'Steen and Leslie Raymer from New South Associates provided general background information on the analysis of bone and plant materials respectively. Cassandra Hill went to great lengths to provide me with illustrated explanations of human bones; some of her drawings are reproduced in this book. Chuck Cantley from New South Associates explained different types of sampling strategies to me. Dan and Rita Elliot are thanked for their hospitality and loaning me books on underwater archaeology. I am indebted to my social anthropology lecturers at the University of the Witwatersrand for teaching me the value of ethnographic observation and theory, especially David Webster, Jeremy Keenan, Johnny Clegg, and David Hammond-Tooke. Tony Greiner from New South Associates helped me generate a site grid map in MacGridzo. Chuck Cantley and Leslie Raymer unselfishly lent me numerous books with pictures of people doing archaeology to use as models. Other people who loaned their books to me or mailed me pictures at very short notice include Jean Allan, Jean Clottes, Tommy Hudson, Joe Joseph, Mary Beth Reed, Tracey Fedor, Theresa Hamby, Tom Wheaton, David Whitley, Marcia-Anne Dobres, Carolyne Boyd, and Jim Keyser. I appreciate the positive words of encouragement from colleagues such as Jacob Turner, Ken Sassaman, Lea Abbott, Courtney Helfrecht, and Erica Sanborn during various stages of the project. Any errors that remain in this text, in spite of the fine guidance provided by the people listed here, are mine alone.

Nancy White from the University of South Florida reviewed the comic book in draft form and offered invaluable suggestions that made this a better book. I agree with Nancy's criticism that it contains too many unfamiliar and idiosyncratic case studies, quite unlike those found in conventional textbooks. My choice of unusual cases is partly due to my training, partly due to my preferences and biases, but mainly a deliberate attempt to move away from the same old examples that have been repeatedly used in other introductory texts.

Last but certainly not least, this comic is dedicated to my wife Sue and our two daughters Debbie and Sarah. Without their patience, encouragement, inspiration, understanding, and help in so many different ways, the comic would never have seen the light of day. Sue helped me think of the main character, Squizee. The name of this teenage girl comes from the fact that she has an inquisitive nature and likes to ask questions. The likeness of the girl is based on my eldest daughter Debbie, who, like Squizee, is eager to learn new things. Near the end of the comic I included a drawing of my lovely younger daughter Sarah and her friend Alyssa, posing as visitors in the museum shop. Squizee's dog Digger is based on Scamper, a former family pet. In tribute to my dad, J. H. N. Loubser Sr., I included a picture of him in front of his favorite Electron Spin Resonance equipment at the Physics Department of the University of the Witwatersrand, Johannesburg.

Otherwise, unless explicitly stated or illustrated, the other characters in the comic are fictional and are not meant to resemble any particular person, living or dead. However, I did try to depict stereotypical characters one might encounter in the profession of archaeology. As a group, archaeology generally includes quite ordinary—albeit slightly eccentric—people, among whom the likes of Indiana Jones or Lara Croft would be hard to find.

INTRODUCTION

It all started in the exhibit area at the Annual Meeting of the Society of American Archaeology in Minneapolis in 1995. A group of fringe archaeologists interested in rock art were milling around a booth specializing in used and antique books, when a bearded man with glasses, Mitch Allen of AltaMira Press, started talking to some of us about what we were interested in publishing. Paging through an early example of a contract archaeology report, I mumbled that the report might have been less dull if it had more pictures. This got Mitch's attention.

I explained that it was not so much that archaeological text is monotonous—there are some excellent archaeological writers out there—but, in my mind, pictures can impart an idea more concisely and effectively, especially in a visual discipline like archaeology. By presenting an archaeological project in a series of pictures, for instance, it would be possible to demonstrate its progression from start to finish. Instead of describing field methodology in all its tedious detail, as archaeological reports always do, why not show a few photographs or realistic drawings of people using the equipment on the actual terrain? Unlike linear text, pictures can magically combine divergent aspects of a project within a single frame. If annotated properly, one picture can succinctly convey information on both the conduct of the project and its findings: crew size and hierarchy, gender make-up, handling of equipment, topography, vegetation, artifacts recovered, and so on. Conventional reports describe and illustrate artifacts apart from their original contexts; a practice that I believe creates a false sense of separation between fieldwork and interpretation. I suggested to Mitch that a project presented in a picture format like a cartoon strip, supplemented by graphs and tables, would effectively show the connection between theory and practice.

After patiently listening to my polemic, Mitch proposed that I create an introductory archaeology book in comic book form for first-year students and the lay public. Professionals in their fields can also benefit by reading such introductory books, even if only to remind them about the basics of their discipline. Mitch was particularly impressed with a comic book he recently read, called "Japan Inc.," which introduced the Japanese economic boom of the 1980s to first-year economics students. The comic has a simple story line with impressive black and white drawings that help explain certain tricky economic principles. After exchanging samples of each of our ideas, Mitch and I agreed to go ahead with the project. This book is the result.

I felt that the comic would be more reliable and convincing if it included aspects of archaeology and prehistoric locations that I have encountered personally. Since I am most familiar with the Southeastern United States, South Africa, and Australia, readers of the comic will notice my bias towards these regions. Because my training and experience is mostly in prehistoric archaeology, or the archaeology of people without a written history, I mostly limited myself to this branch of archaeology, though you will notice that I also address classical archaeology, historical archaeology, underwater archaeology, and other branches of the discipline. The specific setting of this comic is in the foothills, or Piedmont, of Georgia, where a young woman, Squizee, is first introduced to archaeology after looters have discovered prehistoric pots on her father's farm.

You, the reader, accompany Squizee as she assists an archaeologist from a museum, Dr. Holmes, with an archaeological recovery project launched by the discovery of these prehistoric pots. Along the way, she meets the various specialists who help Dr. Holmes analyze the material he finds, links up with a contract archaeology crew, meets a Native American observer, and . . . well, just read on.

Using many more pictures and far fewer words, I'm hoping to tell here not only Squizee's story, but the story of everyday archaeological work as you would find it described in a standard textbook for a college course. And, while these elements are scattered in and around the elements of Squizee's story (after all, this is a comic book), the key topics that are addressed in standard archaeology textbooks are also covered here. Among them:

FIELD METHODS. By-and-large, the story reflects archaeology as I have experienced it practiced in the Southeastern United States. The specific techniques of exploration and excavation used in the deeply stratified deposits of these temperate woodlands are not exactly similar to those practiced elsewhere, say in the dry and shallow desert soils of the American West. Nevertheless, the comic illustrates the systematic nature of archaeological investigation and documents the ways in which archaeologists carefully sample, collect, analyze, interpret, and curate material evidence, much like forensic detectives. The archaeologists in this book design projects, develop a sampling strategy, conduct surveys, shovel test, do test excavations, strip away topsoil, float botanical remains, and wash ceramics in the laboratory. I have attempted to allow you to visualize what these tasks entail, adding a little cartoonist's imagination from time to time. The book lacks only the dirt, mosquitoes, heavy lifting, and endless note-taking of a real archaeological project.

ETHNOGRAPHIC ANALOGY. Archaeological detective work does not occur in a vacuum; to understand patterns one needs a comparative frame of reference. Detectives would be at a loss about how to interpret the clues they discover if they had absolutely no understanding of the society and culture in which the crime occurred. Even though archaeology has its own set of field and laboratory techniques, at the end of the day archaeologists have to refer, directly or indirectly, to **ethnography,*** or the study of living cultures by sociocultural anthropologists, to understand the material they excavate. I continually emphasize ethnography as a comparative framework that assists archaeologists in developing interpretations of what they find. Whereas some archaeologists call this "the tyranny of ethnography," I believe reference to the ethnographic record acts as a constraining mechanism that keeps interpretations within reasonable bounds, especially in those instances where continuity between the prehistoric archaeological record and the recorded

---

* Terms in bold are defined in the glossary.

ethnographic record can be demonstrated. I have seen this continuity myself in Bantu-speaking peoples and the archaeological ruins of prehistoric South Africa, among the Aborigines and their interpretations of contemporary rock art, and in dealing with Native American and Native Hawaiian advisors in contract archaeological projects throughout the United States.

Because prehistoric archaeology borrows from ethnography, it tends to lag behind new developments in ethnographic theory and practice. Developments in ethnographic perspectives, such as evolutionism, diffusionism, structural-functionalism, feminism, and cognitive modeling, have been taken up in archaeology long after discussions of those topics were exhausted in cultural anthropology circles. Nevertheless, prehistoric archaeology deals with a material record that predates the observed ethnographic record by thousands of years, so at times it introduces evidence of societies that do not seem to have any parallels in the contemporary world. In this way archaeology adds to the database of ethnography and challenges ethnographic thinking, even though the interpretive frame of archaeology ultimately hinges on ethnographically informed ideas or paradigms.

THEORY. Archaeology today is a complicated mixture of many paradigms; even though some archaeologists might stubbornly deny holding any theoretical position while others tend to compartmentalize the different positions and then go on to promote some at the expense of others. This comic incorporates these paradigms but certainly does not give each equal exposure. The reason for the unequal treatment of different perspectives stems from my university training and experience in social anthropology, geography, and history. In my graduate years **processual,** or **"new" archaeology**, made an attempt to replace **culture history** studies as the reigning paradigm in archaeological thought. During my postgraduate years the **cognitive archaeology** of scholars like David Lewis-Williams heavily influenced me. I strongly believe that the milieu of colonial decline and the emergent voice of indigenous societies in South Africa at the time facilitated a shift in the direction of what the descendants of the prehistoric people think and say. During my six-year tenure at the National Museum in South Africa, **public archaeology**, including education, site management, conservation, and outreach to indigenous communities and the general public became pertinent issues. Most recently in America, the **cultural resources management (CRM)** industry with its bias towards an **ecological perspective** has been driven home. I present these major ways of looking at archaeological finds in the context of Squizee's project and others.

HISTORICAL AND POLITICAL CONTEXT OF ARCHAEOLOGY. My understanding of the history of prehistoric archaeology as a discipline is that it emerged out of the European Enlightenment and colonization of the world. Whereas the Enlightenment provided the intellectual impetus for Europeans to study cultures and societies from across the world, the actual presence of European scholars in colonies across the world facilitated the observation, gathering, and comparison of information.

Prehistoric archaeology is not only colonial but also has a strong nationalist flavor. It is not uncommon to hear Australian and South African archaeologists argue over a beer which country has the oldest sites or the most rock art, for example. British and American archaeologists seem to vie for the prize for who is doing the most cutting-edge work, both in terms of theory and practice. Meanwhile, French, German, Japanese, and Portuguese archaeologists do some excellent work less visible on the international stage, or at least it so appears to those who read mostly English publications. Formerly colonized countries, such as Namibia, Tanzania, and Zimbabwe, have also developed strong national archaeology programs.

Within these national traditions, archaeologists deal with social issues in their work. Our take on class, ethnicity, and gender issues, for example, influences our work in seemingly subtle but often significant ways, even in the decisions of what to research and what data to collect. And what we find often has implications for our understanding of those issues in contemporary society. The discovery of an African burial ground in Manhattan, the survey of the Little Big Horn battlefield that claimed General Custer, the discovery of royal tombs of women in Korea, all have political implications in the modern world. The political and ethical questions of dealing with archaeology's place in the modern world are ones that archaeologists address daily and are discussed frequently in the following pages.

CULTURAL RESOURCES MANAGEMENT(CRM) AND PUBLIC ARCHAEOLOGY. There is a worldwide trend that is moving away from academic research and excavation in the direction of the conservation and management of cultural resources. The United States model of dealing with archaeological sites threatened by the construction of roads and dams seems to be particularly powerful and effective. Government agencies responsible for funding and permitting the alteration of the landscape insist that necessary archaeological studies be completed prior to construction. Archaeology in the United States today is part and parcel of development projects, with benefits to both conservationists and developers. The projects that Squizee works on in this book are driven by this CRM-brand of archaeology; thus the methods used, problems encountered, priorities established, and results expected may differ from those in the classic textbook, designed to describe academic archaeological excavations of a previous generation.

Intact and visually appealing sites preserved in place by developers are sometimes demarcated and developed as public green spaces. Sites are often set aside because they remain sacred or meaningful places for people whose ancestors once lived in the area. Sensitivity to native concerns is an important component of the conservation concept. When appropriate, the public can visit ancient places to learn more about the past; tourism is thus becoming an increasingly important part of archaeology, particularly when media attention sparks public interest and curiosity. Museums, with actual artifacts on display, cannot convey the sense of place that visiting a site can; though presenting archaeological remains at the site or in a museum setting are also crucial elements of the modern archaeologist's job. No picture or video presentation can replace the experience of being on a real archaeological site. Even the journey to sites, many off the beaten track, requires effort and creates a sense of adventure. All of this is tailor-made for tourism, but it provides new challenges for archaeologists who wish to preserve and conserve evidence of past life from looters and amateur enthusiasts alike, and who must respect native sensibilities. Some of these issues are dealt with here as well.

TECHNOLOGY. With the improvement of technology, such as remote sensing and dating techniques, deeply buried sites can be brought to light, and key changes in society, such as the first appearance of art or agriculture, can be chased further back into antiquity. Technology also speeds up analyses and helps ensure that measurements are consistent. I describe many of the techniques used by archaeologists today to help identify, analyze, and date sites and objects—carbon-14 (**radiocarbon dating**), **thermoluminescence,** ground-penetrating radar, and others. While complex, each of these is best described visually, as I have done here.

Improved technology is no guarantee that good archaeology is being done – an accurate global positioning system reading of the wrong feature only misleads the analysis. Increasing reliance on technology requires that the archaeologists have knowledge of a variety of fields. Since it is impossible to master all of them, it is of utmost importance that archaeologists consult closely with specialists. Cooperation between archaeologists and dating specialists, such as we see in Squizee's visit to a radiocarbon laboratory, is one example of such consultation. The archaeologist's role in collecting a reliable sample for the specialist to analyze is also emphasized.

But physical/chemical methods are not magic bullets that solve every problem. Each technique has its inherent problems and limitations. Data from laboratories are numbers that need to be interpreted just as do other kinds of archaeological evidence. I have outlined some of these problems here and shown how archaeologists try to overcome them.

Archaeology is one of the few disciplines that embrace both the physical and chemical sciences and the humanities; to be effective the archaeologist has to adopt a holistic perspective. Too often, unfortunately, there is a polarization between science and humanities in the discipline. The book attempts to bridge this gap by trying to show that there can be no accurate science in archaeology without a consideration of the human element, nor can there be reliable humanistic interpretation in the absence of scientific evidence.

Archaeological work can be tedious and lacks the glamour portrayed by the comic-like characters of Indiana Jones or Lara Croft. I know that from decades of firsthand experience. Yet it is always in the popular imagination, just like the heroes of comic books. And it has its moments of discovery, joy, learning, disappointment, and excitement.

So turn the page and join Squizee as she discovers the joys and pitfalls of archaeology.

OF POTHUNTERS

AND POTS

Meanwhile, at the nearby farmhouse . . .

Tammy, those stupid dogs are chasin' the chickens again!

Be careful mom!

A decision is promptly executed...

Archaeologists start their search with a research question...

that may lead to meticulous and systematic excavation...

and thorough recording and description of all artifacts and their find spots...

interpretations of which are shared with others via publications, lectures, and exhibits...

while careful labeling and storage ensure that artifacts are preserved for future generations.

Pothunters start their search with trophies in mind...

which almost always results in slapdash and haphazard digging...

and attention being given only to spectacular artifacts...

that are often sold...

only to be forgotten with the passing of the "owner."

Looky here, the man from the museum has arrived!

Hi, I'm Dr. Holmes, and who might you be?

I'm Squizee. My mom calls me that 'cause I'm inQUIsitive. Do all archaeologists work for museums?

Only about 10 percent of us work at museums. At least 70 percent work for **contract firms** who are hired to do archaeology by the government and private developers and 20 percent teach at universities. A hundred years ago most archaeologists were either privately funded or worked at museums. Less than twenty years ago most archaeologists were employed at universities. Now contract firms are where most archaeologists can be found.

Real archaeologists are not the swashbuckling treasure hunters portrayed in the popular media.

They also don't hunt dinosaur bones. Archaeologists deal only with the material remains left by human beings over the last two million years, so even the last dinosaurs —dating some 65 million years ago—are far too early for archaeologists to study.

One branch of archaeology studies the remains of the origins of the human species over the last four million years. They're commonly known as **palaeo-anthropologists**.

Other archaeologists specialize in ancient complex societies that had writing. They are usually known by the culture that they study, such as Egyptologists, who study Egyptian civilization.

Historical archaeologists study material culture of the past few hundred years, both Europeans and the indigenous peoples they met, to complement the work of historians.

Prehistoric archaeologists study and compare the remains of societies that do not have any written language or documented history.

In the absence of written language, prehistoric archaeologists heavily rely on material remains to study the past. Clay pottery, or ceramics, has traditionally been the "alphabet" of prehistoric archaeologists, mainly because pots are common and durable, yet distinctive.

Like baked clay pots, flaked stone tools are able to survive centuries of destructive forces. Stone tools, such as flaked points, are also sufficiently common and distinctive to be used as an "alphabet."

Our understanding of pots and how they relate to human behavior took many centuries to become what it is today. The Aztecs of Mexico, for example, credited old pot fragments with spiritual powers.

European peasants living in the Middle Ages thought that pots grew like mushrooms from the earth.

With the rise of mercantile families in the Renaissance, excavated classic Greek and Roman vases were displayed along with other rare treasures.

The Age of Exploration saw European traders taking the "curious" artifacts of the newly discovered cultures back to Europe as evidence of their travels to foreign lands.

It was not until the late nineteenth century that Europeans started to systematically compare and contrast the pots of foreign cultures. Notions about geological layers (**stratigraphy**), evolutionary change (**uniformitarianism**), outward appearances (**classification**), and comparative cultural studies (**ethnography**) helped these scholars better appreciate differences and similarities among pots and the people that made them.

The realization that pottery from consecutively sealed layers, or stratified intact **contexts**, can be used as markers of time differences and culture change was a major development that allowed archaeology to become a more scientific discipline.

Careful recovery of pots and the recording of their contexts have become increasingly important in archaeological excavations and surveys.

Pothunters normally give little consideration to things like context or recording, thus losing the most important information about the artifacts.

Unlike pothunters, archaeologists are taking increasing care to conserve and store pots for future generations to study, display, and appreciate.

If studied properly and carefully, pots can be used to understand various aspects of prehistoric culture, including the technology of the makers, the function of the vessel, dates of associated objects, cultural affiliations, and even world-views.

By closely and carefully looking at an individual pot fragment, or **potsherd**, an archaeologist can learn a lot about how it was made, decorated, and deposited: clay and temper **inclusion** sources, coiling and firing techniques, design application, and weathering processes.

Squizee, look at the broken edge of this sherd through a magnifying glass. Can you see a fine-grained clay **paste** and a few bigger stony inclusions? The potter probably added the bigger particles as a **temper** to keep the pot from shattering during firing. Lots of things are used as temper—stone, shell, pottery bits, straw, even dung.

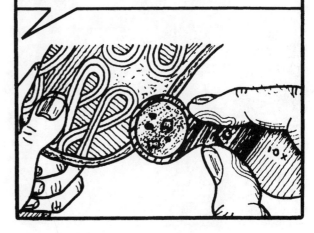

When examining thin sections of the same sherd under a petrological microscope it is even possible to identify the mineral structure of most inclusions. Telltale cleavage lines of minerals can be seen in ordinary light. When viewed between crossed polarizers under the microscope, the clay appears dark and mineral inclusions take on distinctive colors.

Mica
Calcite
Amphibole

Ordinary light

Quartz

Plane polarized light

It is often possible to tell how the pot was fired from microscopic evidence. We know, for instance, that certain crystals only break down at temperatures over 1200° F.

Hey, it's gettin' cold out here, why don't you come on in for supper?

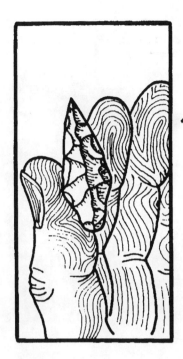

Uh? Oh yes! So far I've been talking about looking closely at the potsherds to find physical evidence about their manufacture. Another avenue of investigation is consulting written accounts of Indian pottery.

Whereas early European explorers in the Americas wrote about the Indians they encountered, they seldom described in detail material items such as pottery.

Later seventeenth- and eighteenth-century French missionaries and explorers recorded some general observations about Indian material culture. The general similarity in their descriptions of those pots and prehistoric pots that archaeologists find is one line of evidence for identifying the manufacturers.

Most of these early accounts were written from memory. It is only more recently that trained **ethnographers** wrote down their direct observations of pots, potters, and pottery users.

Between all these sources, we now have sufficient information to generally understand how Native Americans in this area manufactured pots, called the **coil** and **paddle** method.

Good quality clay is usually located in valleys near rivers. Potters and their helpers collect clay and carry it back to their homesteads in containers.

The clay is sometimes dried and pounded into a fine powder with a wooden club or stone. Large impurities are then removed and the clay is soaked in water.

The prepared clay is then kneaded and coarse sand or bits of broken pots are added until the desired consistency is reached.

By squeezing the clay between her fingers, the potter shapes the prepared clay into long and narrow coils.

The body of the pot is gradually built up by successively adding on more coils. The joints between coils are securely joined together with fingers to make them invisible.

X-rays of sherds can reveal the internal alignment of inclusions, or temper. This helps archaeologists differentiate between coil-built pots and those thrown on a potter's wheel, a technology that was not used in this area but was elsewhere around the world.

The vessel exterior is beaten with a wooden paddle, which could have designs cut into it. The paddle is applied before the clay dries, when it is still leather hard.

Unique design flaws on wooden paddles are transferred to sherds. The occurrence of a distinctive flaw on pots over a wide area helps us track the movement of pots or potters.

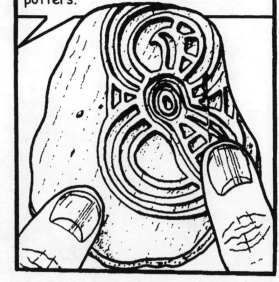

Designs may also be incised into the leather-hard clay. Once dried in the sun, a number of pots are placed in a shallow pit lined and covered with branches, grass, and old potsherds. The grass is lit and the pot fired.

Modern archaeologists fire known clays at known temperatures to learn more about technical aspects of prehistoric pottery. Reddish paste indicates **oxidation**, or high firing temperatures in fairly open fires, whereas gray paste indicates **reduction**, or lower temperatures in more enclosed surroundings.

Hey, what is this in the chicken?

Birdshot! Mmm . . . I now know why the pothunter left in a hurry.

Yuk! To think this bird has been lying in the sun for a day.

Dr. Holmes, why do you think your present observations help to understand the past? Weren't things different then?

According to the principle of uniformitarianism we know that past processes are like those in the present. We use **analogy** to bridge the gap between the past and present.

By means of analogy we know that if a prehistoric pot has a similar make-up to a pot produced in front of an ethnographer, then the prehistoric sherd was likely produced in a similar fashion.

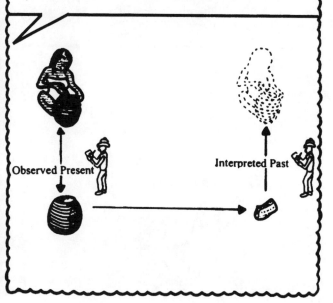

Observed Present

Interpreted Past

Archaeologists interpret the past in terms of processes that ethnographers perceive in the "present." These comparisons, though, are not completely objective, but are very much determined by circumstances of the time. As a result, interpretations change.

During European colonial expansion, ethnographers interpreted societies they encountered as representing different stages of evolution. Influenced by these ethnographers, **evolutionist school** archaeologists adopted a three-stage evolutionary model of prehistory—the Stone Age, Bronze Age, and Iron Age—first used in Denmark in the early nineteenth century.

During the late-nineteenth/early-twentieth centuries, the colonial powers increasingly vied for influence over conquered cultures. It is at this time that ethnographers started to shift their focus on how people, material items, and ideas moved from place to place.

The **diffusionist school** shifted their attention from developmental stages to geographical differences between material objects, like pots, in order to find evidence for diffusion and migration.

Consolidation of colonial control and administration witnessed increasing bureaucratic concern about how subservient societies function. Societies were viewed as systems of different functional parts.

Out of this concern arose the **functionalist school**. The archaeological **processual school** of the 1960s is an outgrowth of functionalism and views objects of material culture as part of a wider system of interrelated parts and processes.

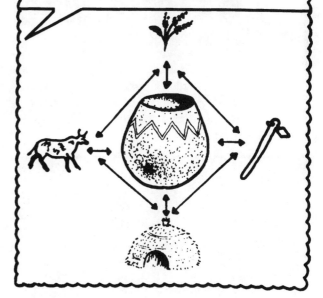

The post-World War II collapse of colonialism and withdrawal from colonized countries was a period of chaos and disillusionment for many ethnographers. During these post-modern times ethnographers critically studied class, gender, and cognitive differences within and between societies.

Once again following the lead of their ethnographer colleagues, archaeologists of the late twentieth century increasingly started to study the class, gender, and cognitive aspects that derive from pots and other material objects.

To my mind if it was not for the colonial experience and exposure to a wide variety of societies, then ethnographers would not have had the opportunity to develop an understanding of shared processes underlying social change and the place of pots. Current archaeological thinking, which is lumped together under the name of the **post-processual school**, is a complicated combination of all these schools of thought. Each approach has its advantages and shortcomings. It can be argued that approaches that are too one-sided, such as **evolutionary** or **cognitive** archaeology, ignore other avenues of investigation. A counter-argument is that being too broad-based or eclectic does not yield insightful results.

These theoretical insights are important because a constant issue that confronts all archaeologists is how to justify and find outside support and funding for our studies. If we're not independently wealthy, we must convince the public of the relevance of our findings. Relevance also comes from a greater interest in conservation issues, such as the best ways to protect sites that contain pots.

We have to see if the site has any research potential before we ask for funding.

To do exploratory investigations, I will need some volunteers To help. Know anyone who might be interested?

I have worked as an archaeological volunteer and photographer.

Very well, if you have the time you can photograph our survey and testing efforts.

Thanks for the bedtime stories, Doc. I'm sure Squizee will make a great assistant.

Huh! Well, uh, sure Squizee can help. See y'all next week when I do the initial walkover and mapping.

CHAPTER 2

A PEEK THROUGH THE KEYHOLE

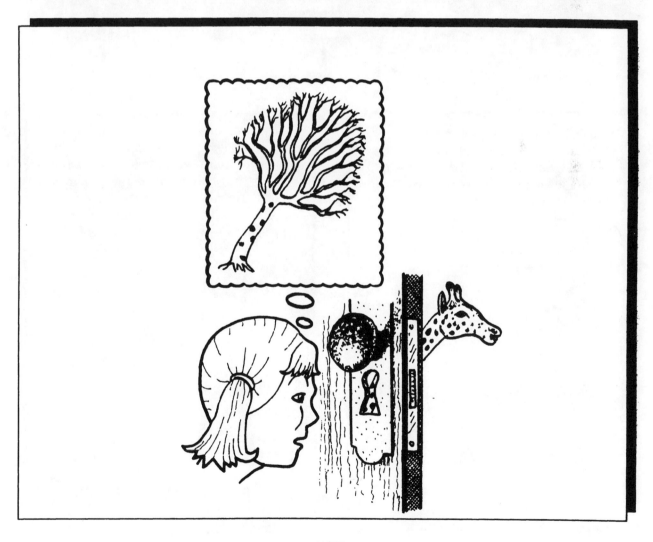

Two weeks later, a large group of enthusiastic volunteers arrives at the newly discovered site . . .

Welcome everybody! Squizee is holding the site map we made last weekend. Let me first update y'all on what we did and tell you a bit about archaeological site survey in general.

We first walked across the site to get some idea of its size and content. The rain last Saturday helped wash away the surface dirt covering various prehistoric artifacts.

That soil erosion made some stone artifacts and potsherds stand out on columns of soil. We did not collect these artifacts but only mapped their locations. We provisionally defined the boundary of the site at the points where no more artifacts were seen on the surface.

Looters discovered this site while pothunting, but archaeological sites can be discovered in many ways, such as by aerial photography. By means of overlapping stereo-photographs, three-dimensional pictures of the landscape can be taken. A famous linear mound site at Poverty Point, Louisiana, was first recognized this way.

Earthen mounds and stone walls often support atypical plants. The configuration of these plants helps archaeologists to identify the shape of sites from the air. Soil discolorations and differences in crop heights also help identify sites from the air.

Unusual ground cover often leads to chance discoveries. Once I found daffodils, not a native plant, marking the location of a buried old historic home.

Archaeologists often discover sites by conducting ground surveys. Systematic surveys encompass walking across an entire designated parcel of land at regular intervals. **Judgmental surveys**, on the other hand, don't cover the entire landscape but focus on those areas thought likely to contain sites.

Once sites are discovered, it helps to record their locations according to the **Global Positioning System**, or GPS. Locked into satellites, GPS precisely locates a site in terms of global coordinates. This helps our ability to find sites again.

The site **datum point** is typically the point from which the GPS reading is taken. The datum point at this site is a rebar driven into the ground at its southwestern extreme. All measurements on this site were taken in reference to this point.

I placed a total station transit instrument, used by surveyors, directly above the datum point. From there I took the first measurement to Squizee holding the staff with reflective prism 5 meters north of me.

After marking this 5-meter point with a wooden stake, I turned the instrument due east to establish the east-west baseline. We now had two baselines, one facing directly north and the other facing due east.

Once the baselines have been established, we applied **Pythagoras' theorem** to establish a third point at a right angle to the two first 5-meter stakes on the base lines. By connecting the first four wooden stakes, we have demarcated our first square on the **grid**.

We then hooked one end of a long measuring tape over the datum point. While Squizee held tightly the other end of the tape, I drove wooden stakes into the ground at regular 5-meter intervals. This procedure was repeated until a grid covering the whole site was completed.

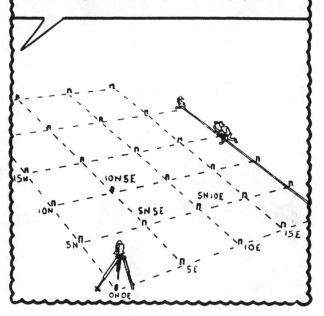

Each stake marks a coordinate point north and east of the datum, expressed in meters, like 50North/25East. This **Cartesian grid** system arbitrarily subdivides the site for the purpose of later artifact mapping and counting.

Artifacts collected from the surface of the site are separated, counted, and mapped square-by-square. The archaeologist can then look for artifact concentrations and empty spaces. This information can be linked to soil types, landform, and disturbances, to give an overall picture of the site.

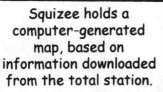

Squizee holds a computer-generated map, based on information downloaded from the total station.

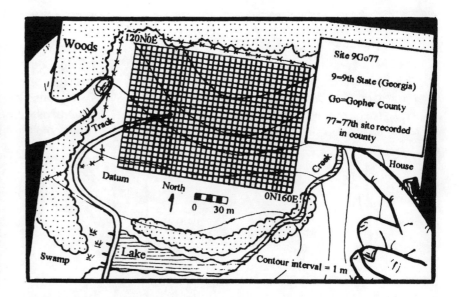

Woods
120N0E
Track
Datum
North
0   30 m
Swamp   Lake
Creek
House
0N160E
Contour interval = 1 m

Site 9Go77

9=9th State (Georgia)

Go=Gopher County

77=77th site recorded in county

On the computer the grid map can be flipped from a top plan view to a more oblique side view.

The mapping software that created a three-dimensional raised contour map can quickly incorporate new information that might be useful to plan fieldwork strategies at the site.

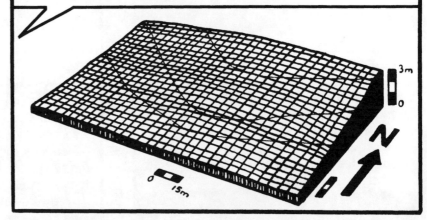

3m
0
N
0   15m

!?

Of course, fieldwork is never this smooth or hassle-free. Look, there aren't even any weeds in this field!

Remember that fieldwork is more than standardized methods and techniques. To conduct fieldwork efficiently, field experience is crucial. So are knowledge of basic archaeological theory and familiarity with previous work in the region.

We have identified pottery fragments similar to those from other sites that are about 1,000 years old. To confirm this site's age, we need to do more work. But just how much work is warranted here? The research potential of the site has to be determined first by further nondestructive work, because the moment we pick up artifacts or dig, we are damaging the site ourselves.

In the spirit of modern conservation ethics we increasingly aim to minimize disturbance of sites that are worth saving. There are even laws about this— **Section 106** of the National Historic Preservation Act mandates that archaeological work should precede development projects where federal money or permitting is involved.

As a result of Section 106, an entire **Cultural Resources Management**, or CRM, industry has developed. A typical CRM project has three phases. These are known as **Phase I survey**, **Phase II testing**, and **Phase III data recovery**. The results of each phase help determine if a site should be preserved intact, excavated further, or if it can be destroyed by construction activities. We are going to start with Phase I today.

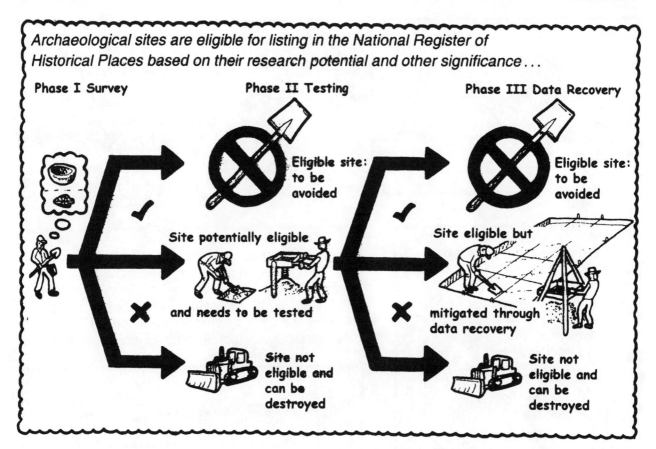

Archaeological sites are eligible for listing in the National Register of Historical Places based on their research potential and other significance...

Phase I Survey

Phase II Testing

Phase III Data Recovery

Eligible site: to be avoided

Site potentially eligible and needs to be tested

Site not eligible and can be destroyed

Eligible site: to be avoided

Site eligible but mitigated through data recovery

Site not eligible and can be destroyed

As I mentioned earlier, the subdivision of research areas into sites and of sites into a grid of squares helps the archaeologist manage and compare features and artifacts. Arbitrary subdivision may bear no relation to buried house structures or pit features, however.

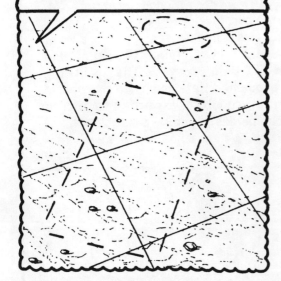

Above-ground structures are often more realistically subdivided in terms of the actual divisions seen on the surface. Southwestern pueblos, for example, are sometimes divided by rooms. When a number is given to each room, artifacts from different rooms can be identified, counted, and compared. In this way archaeologists may learn more about possible age or functional differences or similarities between rooms.

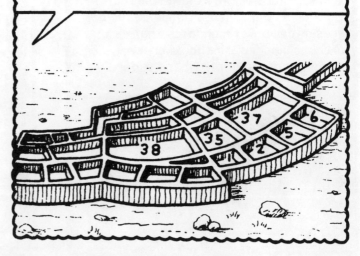

The interior of structures can in turn be subdivided, such as at stone wall sites in southern Africa. Ethnographic information obtained from descendants of inhabitants of a site may help interpret artifacts and their distribution within structures.

The location, or **provenience**, of artifacts we find are just as important as the artifacts themselves, because they help us understand the material in its context. So when we survey the round surface, as we are going to do ow, properly labeling bags containing rtifacts with location information is important. I expect you to do that.

Each volunteer, equipped with plastic bags and markers, meticulously collects all loose artifacts on the surface. Strings demarcate squares within the grid. Bags are labeled according to the southwest coordinate of each block.

The results of the surface grid collection are entered into the computer-mapping program to create various density maps of total artifact count, raw material type, or ratios of pottery versus stone tools. The artifact count helps me produce a conformant, or **choropleth**, map of artifact densities.

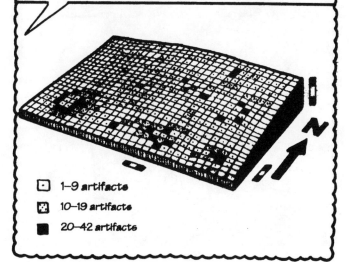

1–9 artifacts
10–19 artifacts
20–42 artifacts

Megan Hertz, a consultant, uses ground-penetrating radar (GPR) to locate buried features, which helps Dr. Holmes plan the next stage of fieldwork.

Ground-penetrating radar is a non-destructive survey technique, one of several types of **remote sensing**. Other remote sensing methods use sonar, magnetism, or electrical charges.

Squizee's dad carefully flattens the plow ridges with his tractor. Smoothing of the ground surface is necessary to make it easier to operate the radar equipment.

Once the area has been smoothed, Megan pushes a mounted antenna along each of the south–north grid lines at a constant speed in the hope of finding subsurface anomalies, such as buried rocks or pits.

GPR surveys are based on the transmission of short wavelength, or high frequency, electromagnetic waves into the ground. The speed of the waves varies according to different electrical properties of the soil. Wave energy is reflected back to the antenna from soil changes.

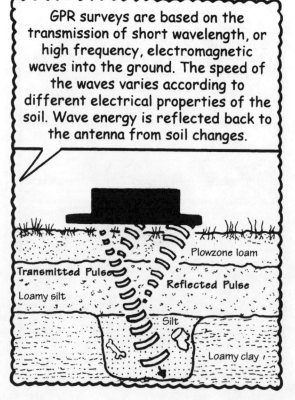

Plowzone loam

Transmitted Pulse   Reflected Pulse

Loamy silt

Silt

Loamy clay

The measure of a soil's ability to respond to electromagnetic waves is known as its relative dielectric permittivity, or RDP. The RDP of dry sand is 5 whereas that of clay approaches 40. The greater the RDP difference between different soil layers, the stronger the reflected signal.

Reflected signals are recorded as a depth profile on a paper strip. This printout is a thin cross section through the soils immediately beneath the radar transmitter/receiver.

Buried features are recorded as hyperbola on the printout. Similar hyperbola on neighboring profiles can suggest a buried pit or shaft. Excavations are necessary to confirm the nature of these anomalies.

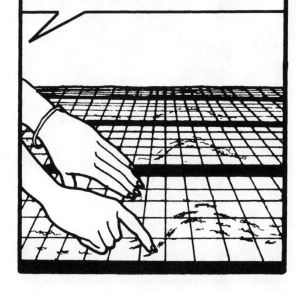

The locations of recorded anomalies are plotted on the grid map. Particularly strong signals came from southwestern and north-central parts of the site, suggesting buried features in these areas.

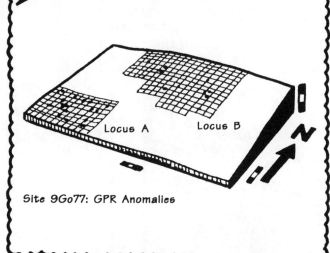

Site 9Go77: GPR Anomalies

Ground-penetrating radar has been successfully used to detect and map buried pit houses and ballcourts through 5 meters of volcanic ash at the sixth-century A.D. site of Ceren in El Salvador.

Now that Megan Hertz has completed and analyzed the ground-penetrating radar survey of the site we can start with systematic **shovel testing**.

Shovel testing is commonly used in the eastern United States with its deep soils, but not in places where soil erosion leaves most artifacts directly on the surface, like western deserts. Using a round-edged shovel and a hand-held quarter-inch mesh screen, shovel tests are dug and dirt screened at 5-meter intervals across the site.

Does that mean we have to test our shovels?

Uh? No! We use the shovels to dig small holes for recovering artifacts and get an idea of soil depths.

Each shovel test has a diameter of 50 centimeters. Shovel tests are dug until sterile subsoil is reached.

Artifacts recovered from screens are placed in a labeled bag. Labels contain information on grid coordinates, depth below soil, and number of artifacts per soil layer.

The location of positive and negative shovel test pits are plotted on the site map. The search for different artifacts from positive tests helps me look for certain patterns on the site. For example, I found that punctate sherds only come from the southwestern corner of the site, whereas check-stamped and complicated stamped sherds are concentrated in the north-central portion.

- ○ Negative STP
- ● Positive STP

The shovel test pit results also help us produce an **isoline**, or contour, map of artifact densities on the computer. High concentrations of artifacts are known as "hot spots" and areas with no artifacts are called "voids."

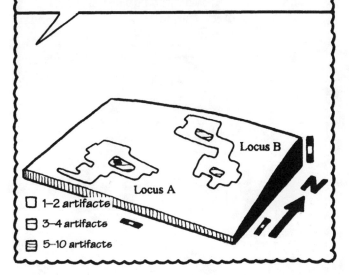

Locus B

Locus A

- ☐ 1–2 artifacts
- ⊟ 3–4 artifacts
- ⊜ 5–10 artifacts

Now Dr. Holmes has the difficult task of designing a sampling strategy for further excavation. Where should he place excavation units to get the maximum amount of information without digging the entire site?

Dr. Holmes can only excavate part of the site due to limited time and money as well as the conservation ethic, which requires that he leave part of the site unexcavated for future study. The strategy of Dr. Holmes' investigation is known as multistage **sampling**; where the whole site is sampled prior to more intensive excavation in certain parts of the site.

The shovel test of the site has been a systematic sample; equally spaced holes were excavated across the site. This type of sampling is fairly straightforward and comes close to an accurate estimate of total artifact values and variety.

However, the regularity, or periodicity, of systematic sampling may match the periodicity of the archaeological record and miss some features.

Probabilistic sampling, which includes systematic and random sampling, enables the archaeologist to use probability theory to evaluate inferences from the sample to the whole site. Such sampling allows a numerical statement of the confidence ascribed to the results.

A simple random sample of the entire site implies that any square in the grid has an equal chance of occurring in the sample. This form of sampling forces archaeologists to look everywhere, not only where they think artifacts or features would be found. Fortunately, systematic sampling at Site 9Go77 has already yielded a reliable picture of where artifacts and features occur.

In random sampling, the location of each test unit is selected by its coordinates from a random numbers table. This sampling strategy unfortunately does not guarantee that all the different artifacts and features at the site are sampled.

On the basis of "chance," certain parts of the site may be heavily sampled and others hardly at all. Random sampling of areas without artifacts may not only waste a lot of time and effort but also unequally sample areas with different types of material culture.

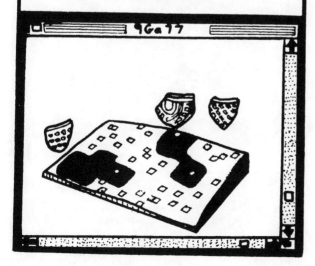

The archaeologist should determine relevant areas to sample in order to clarify important research questions. At 9Go77, sampling of relevant areas may help solve the question of time differences between punctate pots and stamped pots identified in the shovel tests.

*By subdividing the site into relevant areas, or **loci**, Dr. Holmes ensures that both known pottery populations are sampled. This procedure is called stratified random sampling. For this reason Dr. Holmes divides Site 9Go77 into Locus A and Locus B.*

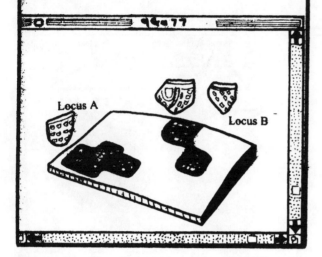

The location of each test unit within each locus is selected from a random numbers table. The larger the portion of the relevant locus sampled, the more reliable the estimate of all pots from that locus. Reliability also increases with the increasing number of units excavated and a decrease in size of individual units.

I get it! The buried anomalies picked up during the ground penetrating radar survey should be treated as a population set separate from the pottery. The possible buried house and pit features need to be selected separately from the pots for sampling purposes.

The anomalies are first separated according to the separate concentrations in which they were detected. Within each area, or locus, individual anomalies are then selected from a random numbers table. With the knowledge gained from the exploratory surveys, Squizee wonders what additional surprises the site has in store for them. . .

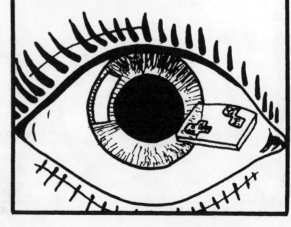

CHAPTER 3

PEELING OFF THE LAYERS

Volunteers set up camp some distance from the archaeological site. Deliberate or inadvertent mixing of modern and old material may confuse future archaeologists.

Meanwhile, from the edge of the plowed fields, the pothunters are waiting for an opportunity to collect some trophies.

I presented the preliminary results of the Phase I archaeological survey to the **State Historical Preservation Officer**, or SHPO, for review. The SHPO agreed with my findings and recommendations that the site 9Go77 shows sufficient archaeological **integrity** to be of value and requires additional investigation, bearing in mind it is threatened by possible alterations to the land. He also agreed to provide matching funds for future work at the site.

Tomorrow we'll start with Phase II test excavations. Let me emphasize the need for care in excavation.

Excavating small and round shovel tests lacks control; artifacts from different layers can get mixed and buried features can suffer damage. Proper excavation is like eating this dessert; layer by layer without mixing the chocolate and vanilla. Mmmmmm...

Careful excavation allows us to distinguish **natural formation processes**, or n-transforms, in the ground from **cultural formation processes**, or c-transforms—the ones created by the people we're trying to study. Ironically, the more sudden the formation event, the better the preservation. The sudden fall of volcanic ash on Pompeii in A.D. 79 is an exceptional catastrophic natural event.

In a surprisingly short time several meters of ash buried this Roman town in southwestern Italy and preserved many buildings and their contents—down to the food on the table. Even comparatively crude eighteenth-century antiquarian excavations recovered remarkably intact material.

A favorable cultural formation event for an archaeologist might be someone else's horrible calamity, a surprise attack on a prehistoric settlement. People are killed, left at the spots where they performed their everyday tasks, and their houses burned down.

The heat of the fire baked hard the clay walls and floors of the hut and charred the wooden posts, allowing it to survive centuries of weathering and decomposition.

Natural decomposition of the bedrock and rotted plant material, together with water and wind action, help form soil. As time passes, soil buries and protects artifacts, house and pit features, and human bone under the surface. Tree roots may disturb some of the archaeological layers, or deposits.

At a later date, people introduce landfill to smooth out an area for later building, an example of a cultural formation process.

Destructive cultural practices, such as war, help modify or destroy the archaeological record.

Modern agricultural and urban developments are particularly hard on ancient remains, especially with the development of modern deep plowing techniques.

In spite of natural and cultural processes of destruction, at least some archaeological layers and material remains have miraculously survived. It is these surviving remains we excavate to learn from, or conserve to save from destruction.

Some special kinds of sites, like caves, transform differently. The natural rock walls and roofs of rock shelters and caves help protect the archaeological deposits that form inside. The comparatively protected environments within caves create convenient time capsules for archaeologists to study.

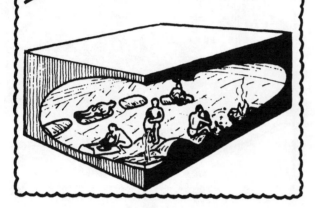

The prevailing humidity and rock chemistry in a cave help determine how long artifacts survive. Dry soils and air tend to preserve organic remains, such as leather, wood, and grass. Alkaline rocks and soils, such as found in limestone caves, help preserve bone. Plant remains often preserve better in acidic deposits.

Given the gradual buildup of natural dust, water transported deposits, and trash, earlier activity areas are eventually sealed below the ground surface of the cave. If natural and cultural alterations within a cave are not too severe, these activity areas are preserved remarkably well.

Because artifacts of a more fragile nature can often be better preserved in caves than at open-air sites, archaeologists typically have to work more carefully to recover the evidence.

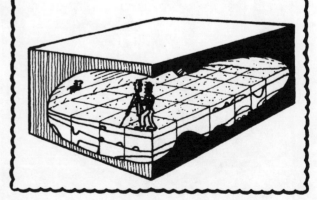

Caves, then, are like books protected by hard covers. The layers are like pages that have to be read one-by-one, while the pictures are features, and the letters are artifacts.

If survey and test archaeological excavations in fields have determined that natural, agricultural, or industrial developments have severely disturbed or destroyed the upper archaeological layers, then there is no need to excavate these carefully.

The crew gets up early the next morning to beat the heat of the afternoon sun . . .

For protection against the heat and sun it is important to apply sunscreen, to drink plenty of water, and to wear hats.

Each of the 21 test units designated for excavation is set out using Pythagoras' theorem. Strings connecting the four corner nails demarcate each 1 x 1 meter square.

Under the watchful eye of Dr. Holmes, volunteer archaeologists use a flat-edged shovel to carefully peel off thin soil layers. First the disturbed plow zone, left by agricultural activity, is removed. Throughout the course of the excavation, care is taken to keep the unit edges clean, straight, and vertical.

The loosened soil is screened through a quarter-inch mesh screen. This technique, known as shovel-screening, is fairly fast and allows for artifacts to be recovered and buried features to be recognized. Notes are constantly kept on soil depth, artifacts recovered, and soil type.

Soil is removed in 10-centimeter levels and artifacts from each level are separately bagged.

Depth measurements are taken from a horizontal string attached to a datum nail in the highest corner of the test unit.

The natural soil layers, or stratigraphy, and arbitrary excavation levels are plotted in relation to the arbitrary datum plane.

Site 9 Go 77
Test Unit 3
100N 90E
South Profile
△Datum

1
2
3
4
5
6
CLAY

0 10 20 30cm

Test units on steep slopes may be taken down in contoured arbitrary levels, paralleling the natural slope of the ground surface.

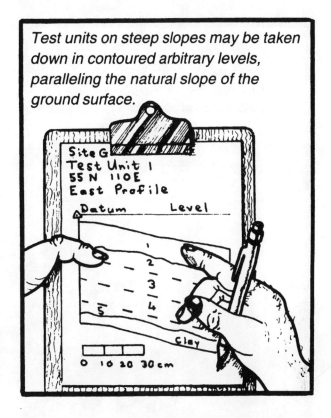

Site G
Test Unit 1
55 N 110E
East Profile
△Datum   Level

1
2
3
4
5
Clay

0 10 20 30 cm

Scraping the exposed soil profile with a sharp trowel and slightly wetting the freshly scraped surface with water make the sediment easier to see.

Color is typically the first noticeable characteristic of soil. Color contains clues about soil make-up and formation. Dark brown soils normally contain decomposed organic matter, whereas reddish soils contain iron compounds, and gray soils indicate oxygen-poor conditions.

The color of each layer can be consistently described with the aid of a Munsell color chart. A color reading is done by viewing soil through holes and matching its color against standardized color chips.

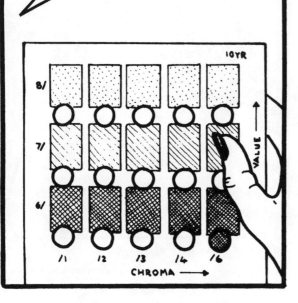

A portable chromameter with a built-in data processor and L*a*b* notation can be used to determine soil color. By placing a measuring tube at a right angle against the soil surface to be measured, the excavator can get a color reading.

Standardized color readings allow different excavators to use a common "language" of colors so there is consistency within and between sites.

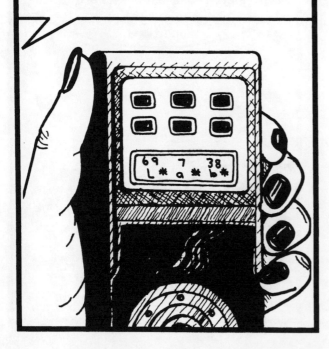

Squizee's task is to keep a record of the excavations; the levels, the artifacts recovered, and the soils. She cross-indexes this information with individual bag numbers.

Soil texture, or particle size, is grouped into various grades: gravel, sand, silt, and clay.

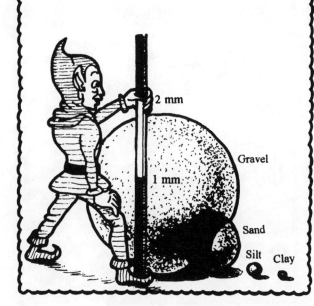

Proportions of sand, silt, and clay can be represented as percentages in graphic form. The presence of particular size grades helps soil scientists, or geomorphologists, understand soil formation processes.

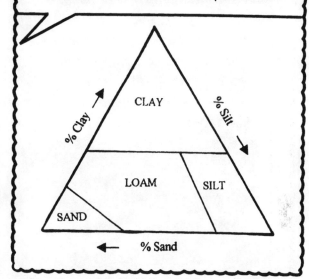

Soil texture is properly determined in a laboratory but the excavator can make preliminary determinations in the field. Moistened soil that breaks when squeezed in your hand is sand. Loam, silt, and clay have smoother textures than sand. However, when squeezed between the fingers, clay forms longer ribbons than loam or silt. Sand is normally indicative of water- or wind-transported deposits, whereas loam tends to be a product of local soil development. Silt-like deposits may occur in features, such as postholes. Clay can be a product of weathered bedrock material.

Soils are often as important as artifacts in telling investigators about past climates, vegetation, landforms, and human activities. At site 9Go77 a typical soil profile includes PZ (plow zone), Ae (light colored leached soil), Bp (buried silt), and C (clay). Anomalies within this succession indicate prehistoric features or disturbances.

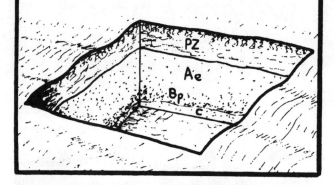

Excavators should be constantly looking for soil anomalies.

This is the time to exchange your flat-edged shovel for a trowel. Careful troweling allows maximum recovery of features and artifacts with minimal disturbance. After all, ground-penetrating radar indicated that this area may contain buried features, possibly prehistoric.

Holding my trowel horizontally I can cut away thin layers of soil. This allows good control and avoids damaging or disturbing artifacts.

Loose dirt covering the artifacts is best removed with the flicking movement of a fine brush.

Careful excavation of complicated stratigraphic layers at sites has not always been part of archaeological practice. Even in the first half of the twentieth century, excavators often used crude techniques to recover artifacts. In the process they missed a lot of contextual information, such as the location of different types of pottery, layers of different age, and pit features with human burials.

Once excavated, archaeological deposits are destroyed forever! It is therefore crucial to get the maximum amount of information from each excavation. Essential to good information recovery is careful excavation—keeping square edges straight and clean—and recording and mapping relevant artifacts and features.

Squizee uses a plumb-bob from a frame grid to transfer measurements of the feature and the artifacts to a grid on paper, working at a scale of 1:10.

Neighbor Alan photographs the cleaned test unit. He uses both color and black-and-white pictures to record the features and artifacts.

It is important to keep a safe distance from test unit edges since they may collapse from weight or movement . . .

Dr. Holmes regularly maps in newly excavated test units with his total station. In this way he can incorporate all newly discovered features and artifacts into the overall map of Site 9Go77. Such a map helps him plan future work at the site.

Excavating numerous small test units across the site helps me get a better idea of the different layers and artifacts of different ages from these layers. Such square units are sometimes known as telephone booths. Phase II work, or testing, typically revolve around the excavations of small square units like these.

Excavating combined units only to the depth where the first features are recognized is known as horizontal stripping. Stripped areas help archaeologists identify structures and household units, for example. Stripping typically occurs during Phase III, or data recovery, excavations.

Meet Mr. Tshilagee from the nearby Native American community. He is here as a representative of the Federally recognized Kadua tribe to monitor our Phase III excavations of features, particularly in the event that we uncover human bone remains or buried grave goods.

NAGPRA, or the **Native American Graves Protection and Repatriation Act**, is a law created in 1990 to protect Native American or Native Hawaiian graves on Federal and Tribal lands, and to provide a way to return the human skeletal material and associated funerary objects in the nation's museum collections to culturally-affiliated groups.

Increasing involvement of native peoples has generated positive and negative responses among archaeologists. On the positive side, such groups have sensitized archaeologists to their religious concepts and burial practices, so archaeologists will treat these remains with proper respect, as they would be expected to in excavating a contemporary western cemetery. But some archaeologists feel that these groups have no connection with very old skeletons that are discovered and should have no claim to them. It is a sensitive issue.

The State Historic Preservation Officer, or SHPO, has reviewed and cleared this Phase III data recovery excavation at 9Go77 and, like federal law state law stipulates, **consultation** with relevant tribal groups.

Archaeologists now take extra care when digging features, not only because features might contain human burials, but also because their contents contain clues as to their function.

The more detailed the feature and its contents, the more careful the excavation and the more refined the tools used.

It helps to handle artifacts *in situ*, in the place of their original discard, very carefully so as not to destroy microtraces that can help explain their function.

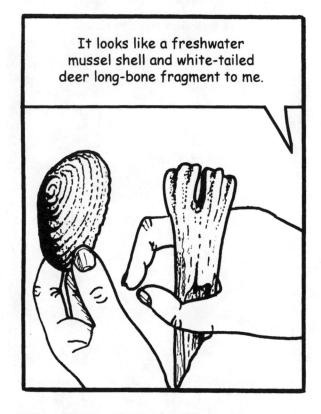

It looks like a freshwater mussel shell and white-tailed deer long-bone fragment to me.

And look— there are more where you are pointing, Squizee. It looks like a buried feature to me. Now that Digger has disturbed the ground we have to carefully excavate the area— and keep a closer eye on the dog!

After careful excavation of the area Dr. Holmes gives a sigh of relief. Finding a human burial would have halted the project while he, the SHPO, and the Kadua group consulted on its proper disposition.

It seems to be a trash pit of discarded shells. The inhabitants of this site must have eaten a lot of mussels!

The alkilinity of the compacted shell within the prehistoric trash-pit protected the associated bone from the surrounding acidic soils. Careful excavation revealed at least two episodes of discard; first shell, and then later bone and broken pots.

9 Go 77
Feature 36
1997

The feature is carefully measured, mapped, and photographed. Artifacts and soil samples within it are carefully collected and their locations mapped.

Measured drawings of features in their plan and profile forms will later be used in reports on the site.

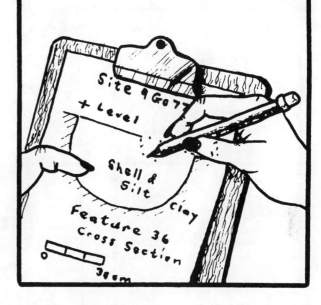

At last Dr. Holmes decides to investigate the area impacted by the pothunters some months ago.

The area around the original hole left by the pothunters is carefully cleaned and leveled to expose the outlines of the feature from which the pots came.

During lunch break . . .

The unfortunate incident moves into the background as the crew exposes a massive soil discoloration.

Arbitrary level units are taken down in a step-like fashion within the confines of the discoloration. Exposed vertical faces, or profiles, help with the three-dimensional delineation of different layers.

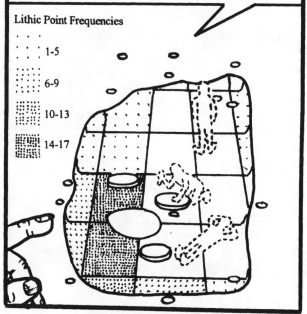

Artifact densities counted per square unit show some patterned arrangement around a hearth. Squizee, I'm afraid it's not a swimming hole, but a pit house.

Lithic Point Frequencies

- 1-5
- 6-9
- 10-13
- 14-17

From other archaeological excavations and the ethnographic record in the United States, we know that the early inhabitants sometimes lived in pit houses.

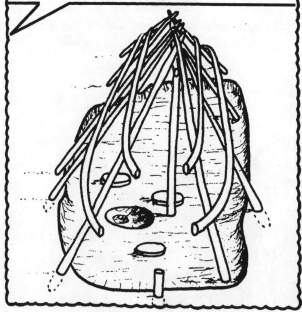

The posthole arrangement along the sides of the depression together with the gap on one side allows us to reconstruct what the superstructure might have looked like.

Many native peoples see old sites as living things with their own internal essence. Excavating these sites is thought to kill them, and may even release dangerous forces whose proper place is within the earth. For these reasons I prefer nondestructive research techniques, such as ground-penetrating radar.

Fortunately, Dr. Holmes managed to raise funds for covering and protecting the excavated features with geosynthetic industrial textiles. These layers can be removed when somebody needs to reinvestigate the features or when a site museum is opened for public visitation.

Let me show you another archaeological site not far from here. It's a cave where a friend is teaching my son how to excavate. Let's drive over to the place.

Thirty minutes later . . .

The cave is down there, next to the river rapids. Archaeologists distinguish between sites from different locations. Our people view them as interconnected: the village on Squizee's dad's land and this cave.

A site does not stop where artifacts stop. I believe people once lived in the cave because of these river rapids. We see the river as a Long Man, with his head in the mountains and his feet in the lowland. The river speaks in murmurs, which only the medicine man, or **shaman**, can understand. The roar of the rapids helps the shaman obtain healing powers from the upper and under worlds.

That mountain over there also links the upper and under worlds. We can have visions of those worlds when we climb to the mountaintops or descend into dark caves. Settlements and mountains do not have clear boundaries; at least not the boundaries archaeologists and administrators try to impose on them.

Supernatural power is everywhere, but is more readily felt on certain mountaintops or within certain caves. These are in many cases our last traditional places of power, so often desecrated by modern development.

In recognition of our concerns about traditional places, the Federal government has created a process for consultation with native groups regarding **Traditional Cultural Property**, or TCP. A TCP is eligible for inclusion on the National Register of Historic Places because of its association with the cultural practices and beliefs of a living native community.

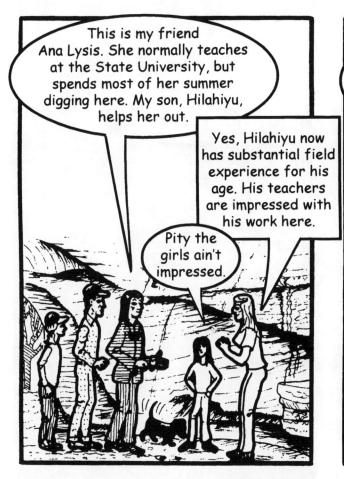

This is my friend Ana Lysis. She normally teaches at the State University, but spends most of her summer digging here. My son, Hilahiyu, helps her out.

Yes, Hilahiyu now has substantial field experience for his age. His teachers are impressed with his work here.

Pity the girls ain't impressed.

The complicated and refined stratigraphy within this shallow cave requires careful and time-consuming excavation, in which removal of soil should be carefully controlled.

We tag, number, and identify each layer and feature soon after exposure. A **baulk** is a wall of deposit left standing between excavated squares to help archaeologists record the stratigraphic relationship between different features and layers.

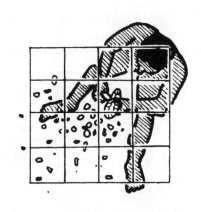

Grid squares help Hilahiyu to record the horizontal distribution of stone flakes. These flakes might have been directly deposited on the cave floor during **flint-knapping**.

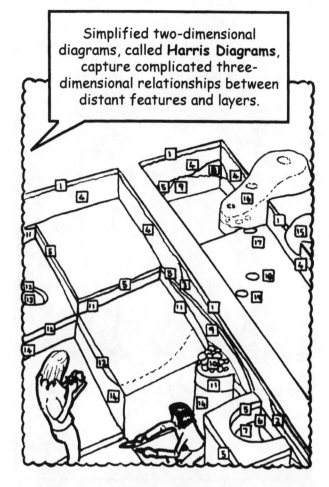

Simplified two-dimensional diagrams, called **Harris Diagrams**, capture complicated three-dimensional relationships between distant features and layers.

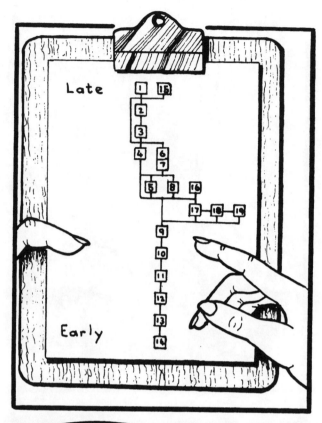

But we can find other clues about the past. Here against the back wall of the cave is an old painting done with yellow ocher. The first Europeans saw it here when they entered the area some 200 years ago. A thin transparent glass-like silica skin that covers the painting probably accounts for its longevity.

The cross-in-ring design on the rock wall is similar to the design on this pot, which is roughly 600 years old.

I think the Old People called that design the Sun on Earth. The cross is a fire made from four pieces of wood. To me the age of the pot is not of much consequence.

Archaeologists almost constantly group material remains according to similarities and differences in time. Archaeologists need to know what material remains were used together during a particular time period. Archaeologists also realize that earlier artifacts and features somehow reflect processes that influenced later ones. Lines of evidence to establish dates of specific artifacts or features are unexpectedly abundant in the archaeological record, ranging from differences in pottery to overlapping features. The challenge of dating is to associate dated remains with undated remains.

Different-looking pots—or other kinds of objects—from a succession of superimposed layers or features can be arranged in a relative chronology, a time sequence in which the magnitude of time difference is not known. An absolute chronology implies that the magnitude of time differences is better known, though does not always give specific calendar dates.

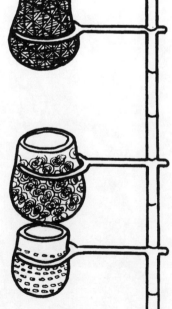

Radiocarbon, or carbon-14, dating is the most familiar and widespread dating technique among archaeologists. This method can be used to date organic remains from around the world using almost any kind of material that was once living.

The method is not without its problems, however. Contrary to popular belief, radiocarbon dating does not provide calendar dates, not in the way that a dated coin or written document would. During your visit here, I would like to explain the basic principles and problems of carbon-14 dating.

Let's start at the beginning. At a height of approximately 50,000 feet above the earth, cosmic rays enter the atmosphere and produce slow, or thermal, neutrons. These neutrons collide, converting atmospheric nitrogen to an unstable form of the element carbon—radioactive carbon-14. Cosmic rays form carbon-14 from nitrogen at a constant rate worldwide.

Carbon-14 unites with oxygen to form heavy carbon dioxide, which mixes with the ordinary carbon dioxide in the atmosphere. Carbon dioxide—both regular and heavy—is uniformly distributed throughout the atmosphere and the ocean; so all living things contain an identical ratio of carbon-12 and carbon-14.

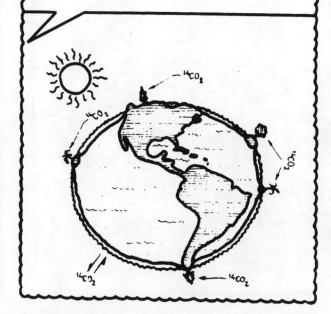

Plants incorporate atmospheric carbon dioxide during photosynthesis. Carbon-14 is passed to animals that eat plants. But when a plant or animal dies they are cut off from the carbon-14 exchange reservoir so no more can be added.

Since carbon-14 is an unstable element, it immediately starts disintegrating back into a stable element—nitrogen-14—in dead material, replacing the lost carbon. In other words, carbon-14 as an unstable parent isotope disintegrates to a stable nitrogen daughter atom at a known rate. As part of the decay process, weak beta radiation is released.

The radioactive decay of carbon-14 atoms is constant and so after one **half-life**, or 5730 years, half the original carbon-14 atoms are left, a point at which daughter atoms start outnumbering parent atoms.

After two half-lives, one-quarter of the original carbon-14 remains, and so on. The age of the dead material is determined once its carbon-14 concentration is compared with that of modern living material.

Radiocarbon age=
$$\frac{5730}{0.693} \times \frac{\text{living carbon}}{\text{dead carbon}}$$

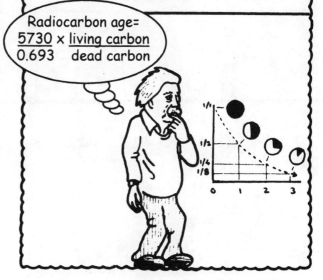

Since this process occurs in all organic materials, we can use carbon-14 dating on charcoal from wood, seeds, animal bones, shell, leather, hair, and even food residues on potsherds. Of all these organic materials, wood charcoal gives the best radiocarbon results.

There are two methods of measuring carbon-14: conventional **radiometric dating**, and **accelerator mass spectrometry dating**, or AMS dating. Radiometric dating counts the beta particles emitted as a result of radioactive decay, whereas AMS dating directly counts the actual number of carbon-14 atoms in a sample.

At this facility we only do radiometric dating. Here we convert carbon samples into liquid benzene. Other labs convert carbon samples into gas. The prepared sample liquid is piped into this scintillator prior to counting. Contaminants in charred wood that would skew the date are fairly easy to remove with acid and alkali pretreatments.

Each beta particle emitted from decaying radiocarbon produces a flash. A photo-multiplier detects each flash.

A modern sample of carbon emits about 8 beta particles per minute per gram of benzene. Older or smaller samples take longer to count.

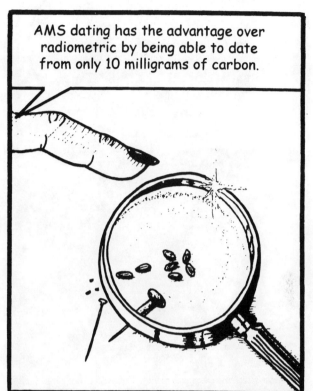

AMS can give us dates from very small samples of important artifacts and so avoids damaging those artifacts. AMS also dates artifacts directly and does not involve assumptions about stratigraphic association between charcoal and artifact. Another advantage of AMS dating is that it is much faster than conventional measurements. However, AMS dating is not as precise as conventional methods and it is more expensive. AMS dating is also more prone to contamination than radiometric methods.

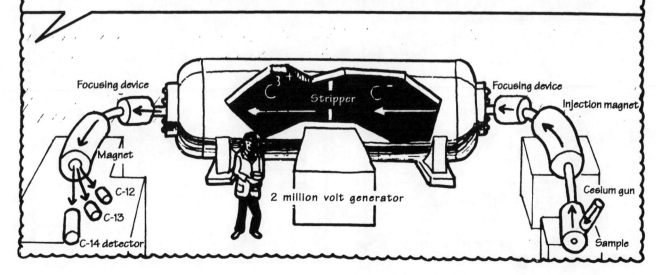

For AMS dating small carbon samples are reduced to carbon in its graphite form. The graphite is mounted on a target wheel, together with a separately mounted control sample. Ions from a cesium gun are fired at the target.

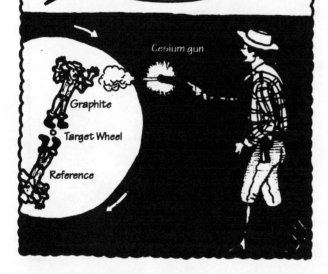

The cesium impact on the surface of the sample produces negatively ionized carbon atoms. A positive terminal within a tandem electrostatic accelerator attracts these ions.

A stripper in the middle of the accelerator takes electrons from the negative carbon ions, leaving them with a triple positive charge. Being stripped of their electrons, the atoms are separated. The positive terminal now repulses the positively charged atoms.

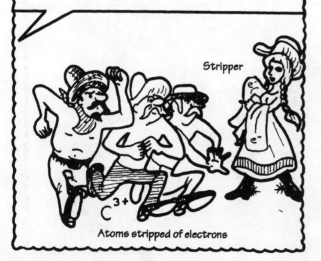

The atoms then pass a focusing magnet. The magnet deflects the lighter carbon isotopes, carbon-12 and carbon-13, away from the heavier carbon-14 atoms.

Having a bigger curve to travel around the accelerator, carbon-14 takes longer than carbon-12 and carbon-13 to reach the ionization counters at the end of the accelerator. The carbon-14 atoms in the sample are compared with those in the modern control sample, and calculated against the half-life. The less carbon-14 counted, the older the sample.

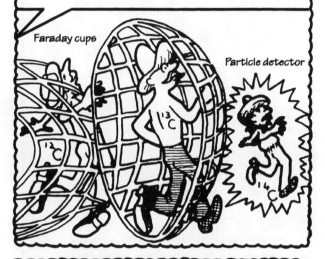

Faraday cups

Particle detector

Raw laboratory dates should not be taken at face value because of variations in the production of atmospheric carbon-14 through time. Variations in sunspot activity and in the earth's magnetic field are thought to influence the rate of carbon-14 production in the atmosphere. Solar flares that distort the earth's magnetic field probably decrease the production of carbon-14.

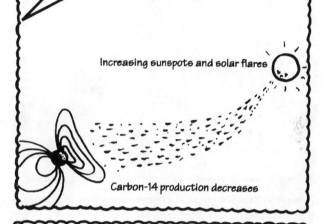

Increasing sunspots and solar flares

Carbon-14 production decreases

Poor atmospheric mixing and the larger oceans in the south mean that there is less carbon-14 in the southern hemisphere.

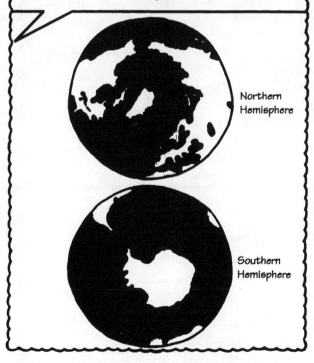

Northern Hemisphere

Southern Hemisphere

In more recent years the burning of large quantities of coal—which has very old carbon— has diluted atmospheric carbon-14, whereas nuclear weapons testing has increased carbon-14 production. These are respectively known as the **fossil fuel effect** and **atom bomb effect**.

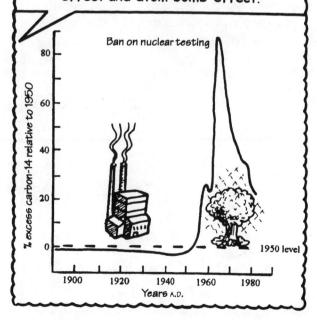

In addition to variations in atmospheric carbon-14, certain plants take up lighter carbon-13 and carbon-12 isotopes in preference to the heavier carbon-14. Corn takes up less carbon-14 than wood and so would appear younger than wood when dated. This differential uptake is known as **fractionation** and can fortunately be corrected after measuring the ratios of isotopes in samples to be dated.

Fluctuations in atmospheric carbon-14 concentrations can also be corrected, or **calibrated**, such as when scientists had to reconcile radiocarbon dates with known dates from Egyptian Old Kingdom coffins.

Ratio of ancient and modern (1950) carbon

Theoretical radiocarbon curve

Known age samples from royal Egyptian tombs

Actual historical age

Because of all these complexities, a modern standard for how much carbon-14 a modern sample should have was needed. The so-called Pee Dee clay oxalic acid standard is used, replacing an original wood sample grown in A.D. 1950. The international use of this standard and the year A.D. 1950 as the zero point of the radiocarbon timescale avoids the distortions introduced by fossil fuels and nuclear fall-outs. All raw radiocarbon counts in the laboratory are quoted as years before 1950, even if an object is dated in the year A.D. 2000.

How do they correct carbon dates?

Trees that consistently produce one ring per year have been central in correcting radiocarbon dates. Bristlecone pines in California have been particularly useful. This has been the work of dendrochronologists, people who study tree-rings.

Matching patterns of annual rings between different segments of wood from both living and dead trees allows dendrochronologists to string together a tree-ring sequence, or a **dendrochronology**.

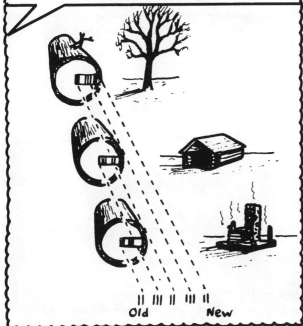

Old   New

Unusually wide or narrow tree-rings that indicate good or bad growing seasons make matching contemporary portions from different trees easier. Dendrochronologists now use microscopes linked to computer monitors for more precise measuring and matching tree-rings. Dead bristlecone pine tree wood can survive up to 4,000 years in some environments and there are live bristlecone pine trees that are 4,000 years old, so dendrochronologists have compiled tree-ring sequences up to 8,000 years long!

By radiocarbon dating tree-rings of known dendrochronological age scientists can determine how well radiocarbon years conform to or deviate from calendar years.

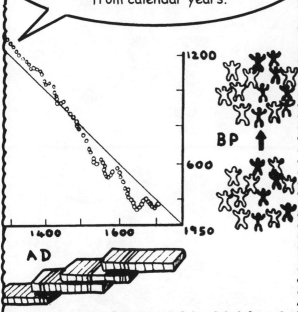

A correction, or calibration, curve is compiled from tree-rings that have been radiocarbon dated. Raw radiocarbon dates from the laboratory are checked against the calibrated curve to compensate for past fluctuations in atmospheric radiocarbon. Calibrated dates are closer to historical, or calendar, dates than raw dates are.

To calibrate a raw date it is necessary to read it off against a tree-ring date. When calibrating dates from the southern hemisphere, 30 years should be subtracted from the raw laboratory date. Laboratory dates are expressed as years Before Present, or B.P. To distinguish them, calibrated dates are expressed as B.C. or A.D., like historical dates.

Due to the occasional wiggle in the calibration curve one radiocarbon date can correspond with up to three alternative calendar dates. To determine which alternative represents the correct date is sometimes difficult.

Therefore you must read radiocarbon dates in archaeological reports with some care. First, some archaeologists do not calibrate raw lab dates. Second, wiggles along certain sections of the calibration curve make it impossible to precisely reconcile radiocarbon and historical dates.

So how do we know if a carbon date is right?

Various statistical methods may help archaeologists determine the best age estimate for two or more dates. One is known as a weighted average. This calculation is best done using raw dates from the lab and only then calibrating the weighted average.

A raw radiocarbon date from the lab is always reported with a ± value, such as 4000±50 B.P. This value is known as the counting error, or **standard deviation**. Radioactive decay is a spontaneous process and the observed rates of disintegration always vary about an average value. This inherent statistical error is expressed as $\pm\sqrt{}$ number of accumulated counts.

The error term means that there is a 68% probability that the true average age lies within one standard deviation from the measured age; in this case, 50 years in either direction of 4,000 years before present. For more precision, you could assume that there is a 95% chance that the true average lies within two standard deviations from the measured age, or 100 years in either direction of 4000 B.P.

1950-4000 = 2050 B.C. Add or subtract 100 years . . . means a 95% chance of the sample being from between 1950 B.C. and 2150 B.C. Then I have to calibrate against the tree-ring curve . . . oh, never mind!

Counting error is dependent on sample age and sample size. The older or the smaller the sample the longer the counting time needed. Counting errors affect precision whereas other errors affect the accuracy of radiocarbon dates. If the bull's eye represents the true date, then . . .

these results are inaccurate and have low precision.

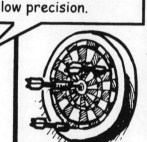

But inaccurate results can have high precision. . .

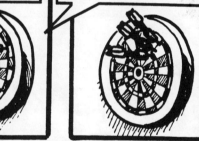

and accurate results can have low precision.

Ideally, accurate results are also precise ones.

Random error, due to varying rates of beta particle emission, is reduced with increased counting time.

Another common problem: Old heartwood from the center of the tree dies long before the outer sapwood and may give too old a date for when people cut down the tree. This is known as the **old wood problem**. Ideally, prior to sampling the research should try to identify and separate heartwood from sapwood.

"Old" Heartwood ~~~~ "Young" Sapwood

Systematic error, due to faulty apparatus, is reduced in well-maintained and updated laboratories.

The re-use of old wood in later structures—a common situation where construction wood is rare— may give far too early a date for the structure that the wood is recovered from.

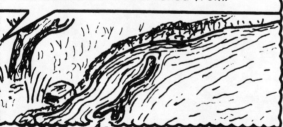

A radiocarbon date of a wooden object that is used for a very long time, like a religious or ritual object, would be too early for its eventual context.

1550   1500   1600

This error is known as **residuality**. All wood must predate the contexts in which it is found. The tree has to grow before it can be chopped down and used. However, archaeologists need to use other evidence to determine how much older the charcoal is than the context in which it was found. Remember, the charcoal will only give you the date the tree died.

Charcoal from sealed contexts, such as from the bottom of a pit feature, would give a more reliable date for nearby objects than charcoal in the topsoil or charcoal from outside the pit. Those would be more likely to be contaminated or brought in after the other objects were deposited.

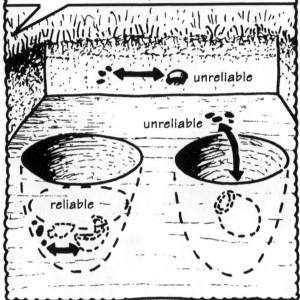

An independent check for the accuracy of radiocarbon dates is the relative sequence of charcoal contexts. Dated charcoal samples from the lowest contexts should have earlier dates than those from higher up, while samples from the same surface should be roughly contemporary.

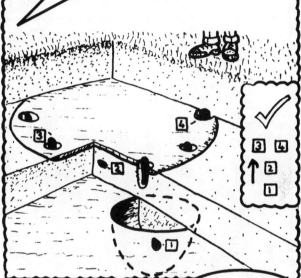

Proper interpretation of radiocarbon dates is complex, and reports of dates should therefore be thorough and standardized. Minimally it is important to report the sample location, weight, identification, laboratory number, raw date, standard deviation, and calibrated date.

The most reliable dates are those supported by independent evidence...

Three AMS determinations from different laboratories showed that cloth bits from the Shroud of Turin, thought by some to be the burial cloth of Jesus from the first century A.D., calibrate to between A.D. 1275 and A.D. 1380. These dates coincide with the first written mention of the shroud in the Middle Ages.

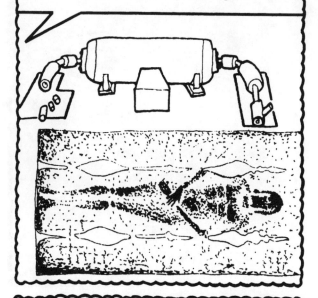

Taken at face value then, the radiocarbon dates and extant historical records suggest that the shroud dates to approximately 1,375 years after the body of Jesus was supposedly wrapped in it. Subsequent high magnification examination of fibers from the Turin Shroud showed the remnants of dead fungi and bacteria. It is possible that these organic remains contaminated the fibers.

The AMS dates from the three different laboratories were virtually the same and therefore highly precise. However, the subsequent discovery of contaminants suggests that the dates might be inaccurate. The precise but possibly inaccurate dates for the Turin Shroud show that is possible to be precisely inaccurate. So AMS dating has not conclusively established a date for the cloth as we had hoped it would.

At the end of the day a disillusioned Squizee leaves the laboratory . . .

a few weeks later . . .

Serious archaeology has never been about treasure hunting. Contemporary archaeology has moved away from the gentleman scholar of the late nineteenth and early twentieth centuries.

Culture resources archaeologists increasingly have to manage people and money.

The challenge to incorporate new technology into archaeological practice has also become greater in more recent years.

Take this electronic clipboard, for example, which allows me to directly enter information on the transect number, shovel test number, soil depth, artifact type, and time period into a computer database.

TRANSECT #
SHOVEL TEST #
LEVEL #
ARTIFACT TYPE
TIME PERIOD

The grouping of artifacts into types helps archaeologists to order them in time and space. Associated radiocarbon dates have shown that the time differences between projectile point types are far greater than, say, the time differences between different types of computer monitors.

 EARLY   LATE

An **artifact type** constitutes a combination of distinguishing characteristics, or **attributes**, such as side form, base form, and notching. Many different types are possible, and the recurrent co-occurrence of specific attributes on certain projectile points from a particular area constitutes a type.

Reliable radiocarbon dates associated with projectile points from previously excavated sites help archaeologists to order projectile points from this survey into a relative chronology. This is known as **cross dating.**

3000 B.P.

8000 B.P.

9000 B.P.

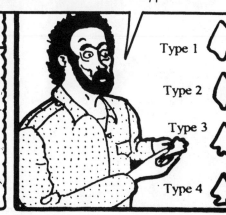

Type 1

Type 2

Type 3

Type 4

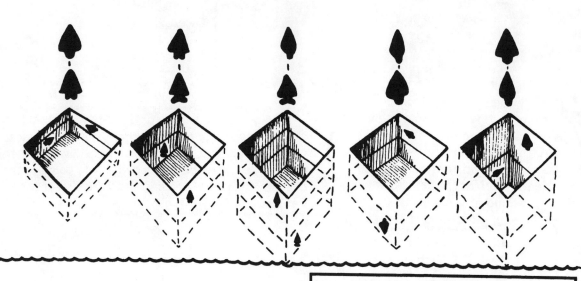

The direct stratigraphic relationship, or **superpositioning**, of types help archaeologists order types in a time framework, or **sequence**. Older types will be at lower levels in an excavation, more recent types at higher levels. Soil scientists can help to evaluate the integrity of stratigraphic profiles and the amount of postdepositional disturbance, which can mess up the sequence.

Repeated observations of direct stratigraphic relationships between types across a region help archaeologists construct an overall master sequence of types. This relative sequence, or **stratigraphic seriation**, must be used with other dating methods to get a historical date. The relative sequence shows only the relationship of artifact types to each other, not to the calendar.

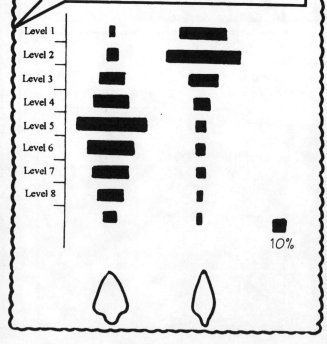

Types that appear contemporary in terms of relative stratigraphic seriation may prove to be sequential in terms of frequency seriation; artifact popularity changes through time.

Level 1
Level 2
Level 3
Level 4
Level 5
Level 6
Level 7
Level 8

10%

The changing frequency of types may show that they gradually gain popularity, reach a peak in popularity, and then fade away. This trend produces a battleship-like curve. **Battleship curves** could be misleading, since small samples or stratigraphic mixing may create patterns that aren't really there.

A few days later Chief and his crew travel to Ghost Town, an abandoned nineteenth-century site. This historic period site is now located on an island in the river and will be flooded once the dam has been built.

Old maps and documents tell us a lot about Ghost Town, but do not tell us everything. Artifact types from the excavation show these historical archaeologists that the site was occupied longer than previously thought.

Maps and books suggest that the town was abandoned by 1850, whereas historical artifacts from these postholes and pit features show that someone was living in this house between 1850 and 1900.

For example, a pipe bowl from the fill of a posthole provides an earliest possible date, or **terminus post quem**, for the posthole feature.

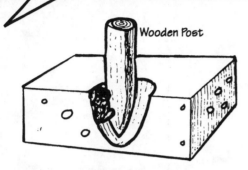

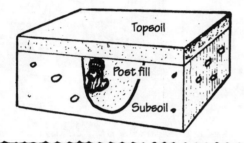

After all, if the pipe was inside the hole, the hole must have been dug after the pipe was made. If we can date the pipe bowl, we know the earliest possible date the hole was dug and the house built. Written records won't always give us those answers because people didn't always write this information down and, if they did, it is usually not preserved.

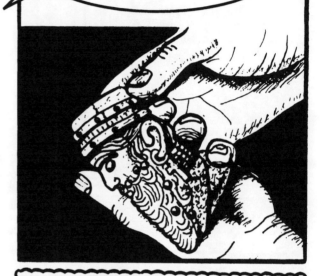

This pipe bowl is of a kind seen in French catalogs that postdate 1850. Manufacturing marks and type of material can also be used to date historic period artifacts. Once we know the industrial center of manufacture and when they were in use, it is possible to place minimum and maximum dates on a historic period artifact like this.

Further proof for the manufacture date of this pipe bowl is that its design is based on ancient Mesopotamian statues first unearthed in Iraq in the 1840s and published in 1850. The design would not have been known in France or America prior to the discovery of the statues.

So how do you know that other pipe bowls like this one are not recent replicas or fakes?

There is a scientific technique that dates baked clay directly without having to destroy too big a portion of the artifact. This technique is known as **thermoluminescence**, or TL dating.

First a small fragment obtained from an unobtrusive portion of the baked clay artifact is ground down to remove the outer crusts.

The fragment is then crushed in an agate mortar and the mineral inclusions are removed with a magnetic separator, screened, and treated with hydrofluoric acid. Typically only quartz grains remain intact.

Approximately 6 mg of crushed quartz is heated to 500° C for 25 seconds within a light-tight container. The light emitted from the heated quartz is plotted against temperature on an X-Y recorder.

Pulse amplifier

Light-tight container

Photo multiplier

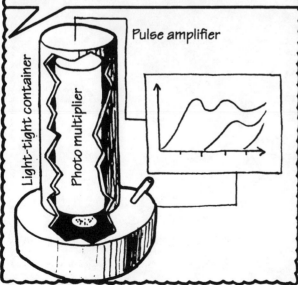

Curve N is the natural glow curve. Curve T is the non-TL light recorded during a second heating. Crushed quartz from a second sherd is exposed to a known dose of β radiation and then heated. This yields a third curve known as N + β. Above 300° C the ratio between curves N and N + β should be constant to indicate that no postexcavation changes occurred.

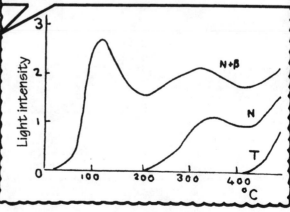

In nature, clay contains minute quantities of radioactive uranium and thorium that emit alpha (α), beta (β), and gamma (γ) particles. These particles attack paired electrons found in bigger quartz inclusions within the clay.

The radioactive particles knock the electrons out of place, producing unpaired electrons.

An impurity in the quartz crystal lattice captures the unpaired electron. A trapped electron and a hole are formed. The older the clay, the more electrons are trapped.

Heating of the clay in making the pot causes the impurity to release the trapped electrons. Recombination of the paired electrons releases light. When heated, older samples release more trapped electrons and so produce more light.

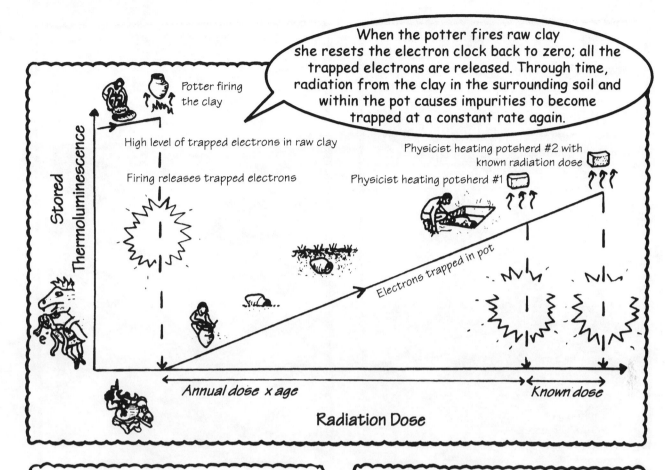

When the potter fires raw clay she resets the electron clock back to zero; all the trapped electrons are released. Through time, radiation from the clay in the surrounding soil and within the pot causes impurities to become trapped at a constant rate again.

Stored Thermoluminescence

Potter firing the clay

High level of trapped electrons in raw clay

Firing releases trapped electrons

Physicist heating potsherd #2 with known radiation dose

Physicist heating potsherd #1

Electrons trapped in pot

Annual dose x age

Known dose

Radiation Dose

The annual radiation dose received by the pot from the surrounding soil is determined by measuring the uranium and thorium concentrations in the fired clay and in the surrounding soil. A small capsule with radiation sensitive material is buried in the soil to measure the soil's radioactivity. Then, in the TL lab, we release the light-emitting electrons a second time.

Since we know how much radiation is produced by the soil, that, plus the amount emitted from the pot allows us to calculate the age of the object, using this formula:

$$\text{Age (years)} = \frac{\text{stored TL or number of trapped electrons}}{\beta \text{ radiation sensitivity of clay} \times \text{annual radiation dose}}$$

Simply because we have written documents on a historic site does not mean that archaeology is not necessary. Even events such as burials have not always been properly documented in historic times. The careful excavation of historic period burials can give us a lot of information, including a rough date of internment.

The radiocarbon method can directly date the protein fraction in bone, also known as **collagen**. Unfortunately, bone collagen degrades and becomes contaminated. Also, the radiocarbon method is ineffective for dating any material younger than A.D. 1800. For these reasons alternative methods are sought to date historic period skeletons.

Electron Spin Resonance, or ESR, is suitable to date tooth enamel. ESR is related to TL dating in that it measures the trapped electron population that has built up since time zero. Time zero for ESR is when crystals first formed within the tooth enamel, when the subject was alive.

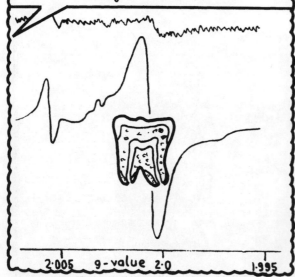

2·005   g-value 2·0   1·995

Powdered tooth enamel is cooled within a container of liquid nitrogen and placed between two magnets. The magnetic field changes until the resonating electrons absorb the maximum amount of electromagnetic power. Electronic processing represents the absorption as a curve; the greater the peaks the more the trapped electrons and the older the sample.

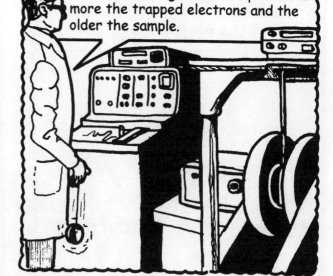

TL dating of baked ceramic heads from the Nok culture in western Africa has shown that the heads are part of a surprisingly long tradition.

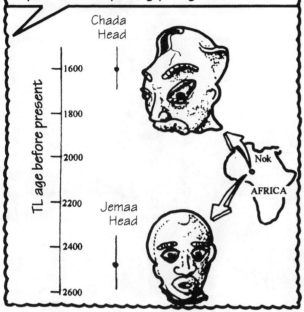

ESR dating of tooth enamel from skulls in Israel have shown that the oldest modern humans *(Homo sapiens sapiens)* there predate the oldest Neanderthals *(Homo sapiens neanderthalensis).*

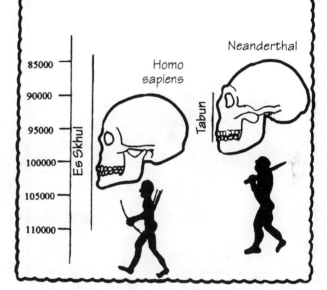

That weekend . . .

Archaeological fieldwork does not pay much and can be monotonous, but it takes me to unusual places and gives me the opportunity to enjoy nature.

WHAT!?

Believe it or not, a portion of Ghost Town was submerged when the river was dammed in 1954. Fine-grained sediments in the lake partially buried artifacts and features. It is my job as a trained **underwater archaeologist** to carefully expose and properly record the submerged artifacts and features.

Underwater archaeologists work much in the same way as their colleagues on land, but they need specialized training and experience with diving equipment and safety measures. Underwater excavations have to be planned carefully since divers can stay submerged for only four hours. Poor visibility normally limits the scope of survey and photography under the water.

Considering that water covers over 70 percent of the earth's surface, it is perhaps not surprising that divers have made some unusual archaeological discoveries.

In 1991 a professional diver accidentally discovered prehistoric rock art paintings in a cave, known as Cosquer, near Marseilles in southern France.

A series of reliable radiocarbon AMS dates of pigment in Cosquer Cave shows that the rock art was painted between 18,000 and 27,000 years ago. This was during the last Ice Age, or Pleistocene, when woolly mammoths still roamed the countryside outside the cave.

With the rise in sea levels over the past 10,000 years, the cave entrance was submerged. It is only with the development of modern diving technology that people were able to reach the cave again.

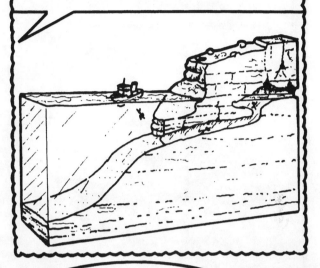

Geological traces of massive glaciers are indicative of the Ice Age. At that time the sea level was much lower than today. Ocean water was locked in glaciers until global warming melted the ice, causing a worldwide rise of sea levels.

The extent of glaciers can be found in certain rock features. Evidence for low sea levels is confirmed by underwater archaeologists, who have found sites from this period on submerged continental shelves. With the melting of the glaciers and the rise of sea levels, these sites were submerged. Dating evidence for such widespread change is convincing, simply because the different pieces in this giant jigsaw puzzle fit together so neatly.

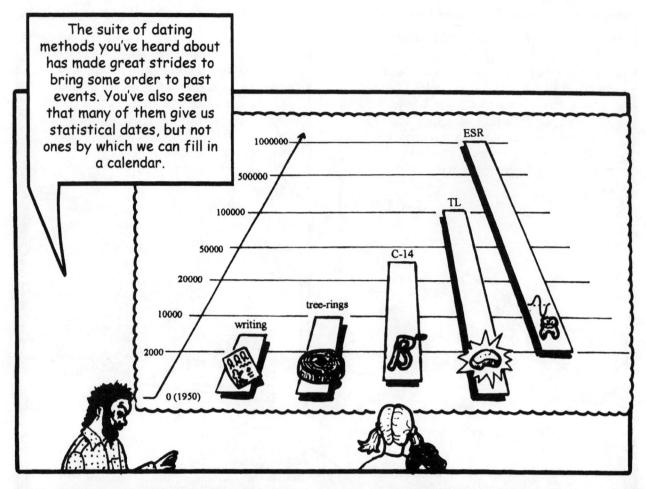

The suite of dating methods you've heard about has made great strides to bring some order to past events. You've also seen that many of them give us statistical dates, but not ones by which we can fill in a calendar.

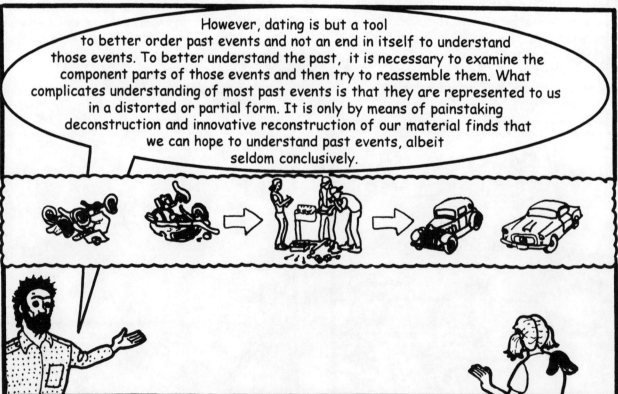

However, dating is but a tool to better order past events and not an end in itself to understand those events. To better understand the past, it is necessary to examine the component parts of those events and then try to reassemble them. What complicates understanding of most past events is that they are represented to us in a distorted or partial form. It is only by means of painstaking deconstruction and innovative reconstruction of our material finds that we can hope to understand past events, albeit seldom conclusively.

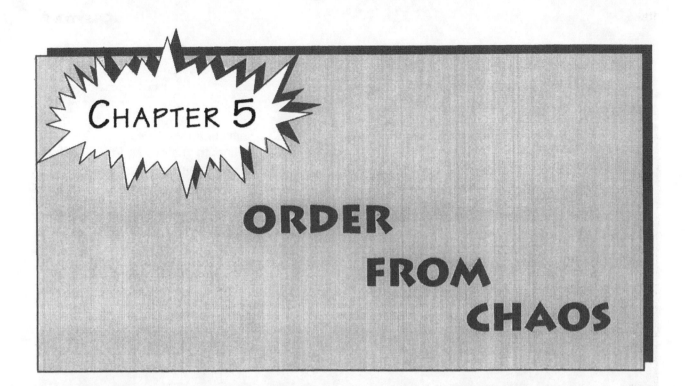

CHAPTER 5

ORDER FROM CHAOS

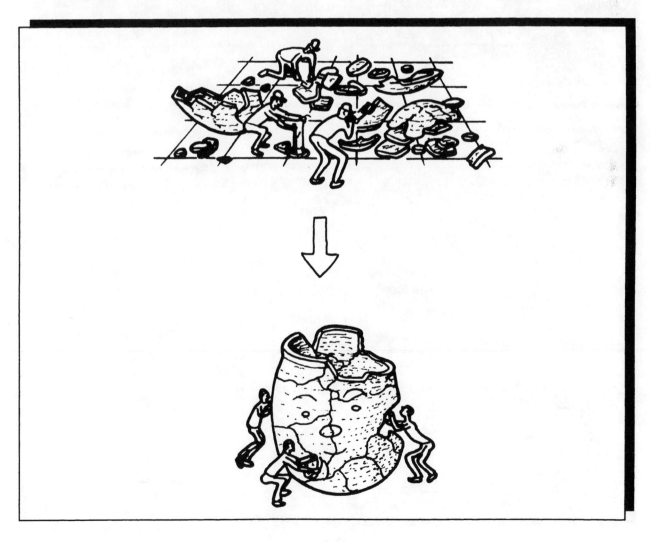

The excavations at 9Go77 and Ghost Town are finished and most of the crew has moved on to other projects. The crew chiefs and a small crew carefully return boxes containing bags with pottery, stone tools, bones, soils, notebooks, maps, drawings, and photographs to the laboratory.

Excavated objects can be damaged or destroyed if they are not packed or transported carefully. To protect a fragile pot from shock and vibration it helps to surround it with soft packing material. Wrapping the boxes in blankets helps to cushion the artifacts.

First, artifacts are carefully removed from their bags. Care is taken not to mix artifacts from different locations. The most important information about any object is its context. If that information is lost or compromised, the object loses much of its research value. So handling the notebooks, photos, and identifying tags with care is as critical as handling the objects themselves.

The laboratory is where the jumble of excavated material is reconfigured into an ordered, published form. Here archaeologists wash, label, identify, sort, analyze, count, draw, photograph, and curate excavated remains. On average, for every hour of fieldwork, three hours are spent in the laboratory and in the write-up of results.

Most artifacts, though not all, are then washed. Dirt on artifacts from well-sealed contexts may contain microtraces of organic materials that can identify the function of the artifact. Some objects are too fragile for washing.

Washed artifacts are placed on drying racks with identifying markers so as not to mix them with artifacts from other locations.

A small rectangle is painted on each artifact with white acrylic paint. Edges of artifacts or areas that contain surface treatments or usage marks that can help identify function or manufacturing techniques are avoided.

The horizontal and vertical location of the artifact is written on the rectangle with a fine-tipped pen. A clear layer of acetate covers the dried ink.

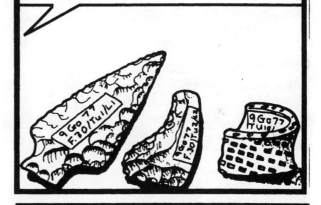

Once labeled, artifacts can be moved around the lab without fear of losing information about their context.

When refitting broken ceramic pots it is best to use glues that can be removed by acetone so that any mistakes can be fixed without causing new breakage.

We do not always need a whole object to know what it looked like. Knowing the rim diameter and curvature of a sherd is often enough to determine the size and shape of a pot.

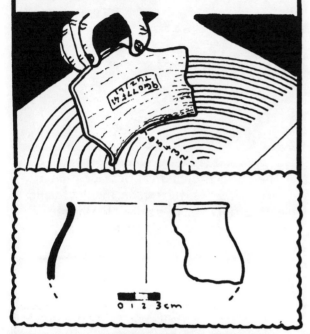

The reconstruction of a whole artifact from a fragment is based on knowledge of complete examples. But not all fragments suggest the entire shape of an artifact. Tips of stone tools are less useful than basal fragments, for example.

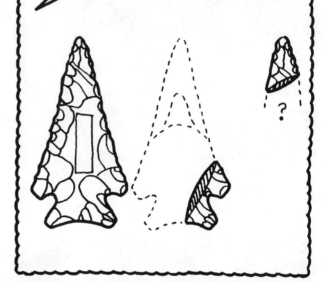

Artifact measurements and other information are entered directly into the computer. This allows vast amounts of information to be sorted, grouped, and counted, and then presented in tables, graphs, texts, and pictures.

Archaeologists devote many hours of hard and monotonous work entering this information. The payoff in usable information for analysis and interpretation may only be available years later.

Drawing artifacts strengthens an archaeologist's observational powers, and highlights aspects relevant to identification and interpretation. Drawings can depict both easily visible and more faint surface areas. All illustrations should contain a metric scale.

Good photographs of artifacts constitute evidence that can be universally understood and verified. Typically, artifacts from similar periods or types are photographed together. The light source is normally in the upper left-hand corner. All photographs should include a metric scale.

Location information, or provenience, is entered on every artifact. This allows an archaeologist to relocate artifacts on the excavated site and reconstruct its context in relation to structures and other artifacts.

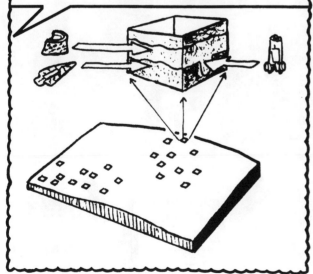

As principal investigator, Dr. Holmes is leading a group of archaeologists to study the material found at 9Go77 and Ghost Town.

Armed with appropriate analytical skills and theoretical backgrounds, each team member is ready to write about the who, what, where, when, why, and how of the excavated remains...

Ana Lysis: Prehistoric Lithics

Dr Holmes: Prehistoric Ceramics

Ed Dibble: Plant Remains

Madchen Knochen: Bone Remains

Chief: Historic Artifacts

Dr. Holmes shares with Ana Lysis, the lithics specialist, some of the research questions that need to be addressed in the analysis and interpretation of stone tools from 9Go77.

No artifact can be fully described. For example, a stone point can be viewed from a great number of angles, each yielding different information, and this does not even include possible studies at the molecular level.

Some archaeologists postulate an ascending scale of difficulty and an inverse scale of confidence in interpreting artifacts. According to them, questions about material elements, such as technology and subsistence, logically precede questions concerning more abstract concepts of society and ideology.

Other archaeologists view questions about technology, subsistence, society, and ideology as interconnected; knowledge concerning the one cannot be complete without at least some knowledge about the others.

Lithics are the most durable artifacts in the archaeological record and archaeologists have spent a lot of time and ingenuity studying them. Basic laboratory analyses include rock identification, manufacturing methods, and use-wear. Siliceous, or glass-like, rocks make the best cutting tools and were often traded over great distances by those who needed them. These include: volcanic glass, or **obsidian**; baked limestone, called **chert** or **flint**; and quartzite, or altered sandstone.

What can you learn from these rocks anyway?

Methods of manufacture can be inferred from flakes on stone tools, actual observations of production among living communities, and experiments by archaeologists to replicate ancient toolmaking processes.

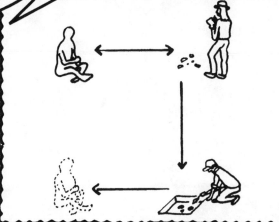

The first step in the production process is to directly deliver a blow to a rock known as a core and so create a primary flake.

A number of features on a flake made by a person help to distinguish it from naturally fractured ones.

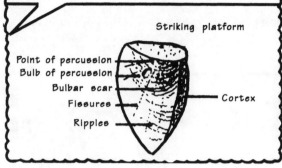

Secondary flakes are then removed from the primary flake with a sharp blow placed immediately behind the edge of the primary flake.

Finally a point of bone or antler is pressed against the stone edge. This **pressure flaking** removes thin and narrow flakes. The production of lithics creates a lot of trash. These by-products of lithic production are known as **debitage**.

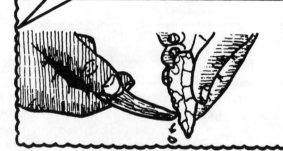

A standard terminology, or **nomenclature**, developed by many researchers over a long period of time helps archaeologists to describe different parts of lithic points.

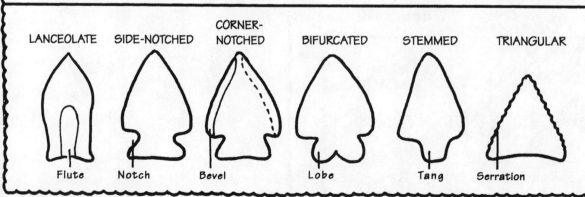

Archaeologists sometimes use statistical summary descriptions when dealing with a great number of artifacts. For example, **linear regression statistics**, or sum of the least squares, can be used to show the relationship between lithic point size and depth below ground.

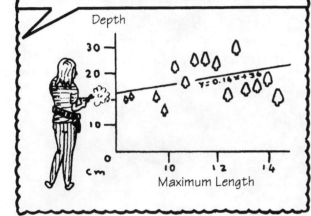

One problem with the use of statistics in archaeology is that the size of the overall population from which a sample is taken is not known, a basic condition required by statisticians. Moreover, units of measurement may accentuate or obscure patterns. Tests of significance give a measure of validity to the use of statistics for detecting patterns. But use of statistics in archaeology is far more controversial, and more often contested, than in economics or opinion polling.

Squizee and Amitai attempt to replicate the process by which stone tools were used for Ana Lysis so she can compare the use wear patterns, the traces of functional activities left on the stone tool itself, with those found on prehistoric lithics. This kind of work is known as experimental archaeology.

Ana Lysis carefully examines prehistoric artifacts for microwear traces. On even the hardest of stones she can identify the bright and smooth marks left by Squizee's woodworking or the dull and pitted edges created by Amitai in scraping hides.

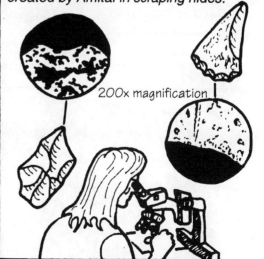

200x magnification

This is another element that differentiates archaeologists from other scientists. Scientists can control and repeat their experiments over and over under laboratory conditions. Duplication is not possible when dealing with the activities of prehistoric people across different cultures.

How did you fit those people in these tubes?

Archaeologists may conduct experiments addressing questions concerning efficiency, for example, when in fact this is a relative concept. Aboriginal men from northern Australia, for instance, prefer quartz to chert, even though chert is locally abundant and easier to flake.

These Aborigines believe that the special glow in quartz has spiritual qualities that helps them kill game. Scientists know this glow as piezoelectricity, or pressure luminescence. The almost universal preoccupation of nonindustrial cultures with the spiritual power of things is different from the strictly functional perspective of many Eurocentric archaeologists.

I think that a Eurocentric emphasis on technology and production has clouded archaeological thinking about things like ideology in other cultures. Ironically, it is ideological notions instead of technology that normally stay the same over millennia. Given the right contexts and methodology, archaeologists can sometimes reconstruct the ideological system behind artifacts better than they can the actual technology.

I guess what you said also applies to pottery and other artifacts. But we should not lose sight of our inevitable tendency to place objects into groups. It is imperative to know what belongs together and what does not.

Doesn't everybody do that?

This brings us to classification, or **typology**. Archaeologists classify artifacts into rigid types to help them get a better grip on time, cultural, or functional differences. This classification from outside is called **etic**. People who actually make the artifacts normally classify artifacts according to a variety of different criteria, such as the status, gender, or ethnic affiliation of the consumer. This indigenous classification is known as **emic**.

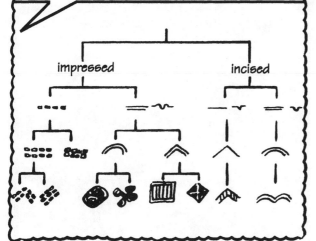

Etic classification can be divided into taxonomic and multidimensional classifications. Taxonomic classification usually involves organizing the typology around one dimension, such as decoration, and breaking it into increasingly specific units.

impressed   incised

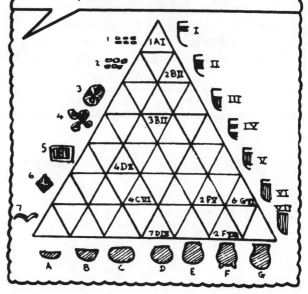

Multidimensional classifications are derived from the specific intersection of three or more distinctive dimensions, such as decoration, vessel shape, and placement of decoration.

The most successful classifications are those that consistently separate types in accordance with the contexts they come from, assuming, of course, that the contexts are reliable.

Types that share a set of characteristics should eventually separate out spatially or chronologically from those that share another set of characteristics.

A group of pottery types that share a distinctive set of characteristics is known as a ceramic culture. Sites with material reflecting only one culture are known as **single-component sites**, whereas those possessing more than one culture are **multi-component sites**. A ceramic culture is typically named after a modern town or place where it was first identified.

The Cartersville and Swift Creek ceramic cultures are but two of many such cultures in the Southeastern U.S. When observed on a regional scale, the spatial and chronological distribution of these cultures becomes apparent.

A collection of contemporaneous ceramic types at a site is known as an **assemblage**. Roughly contemporary assemblages from a group of sites within a region combine to form a **phase**. Related phases through time form a tradition. **Facies** are regionally distinct but contemporary phases within a tradition.

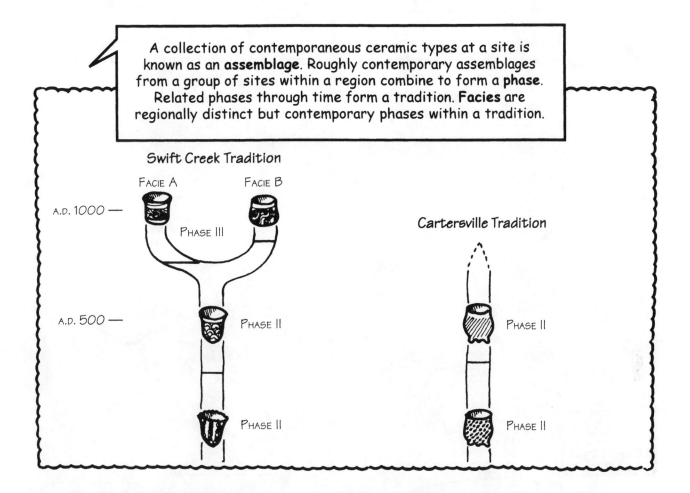

Swift Creek Tradition

FACIE A   FACIE B

A.D. 1000 —

PHASE III

A.D. 500 —   PHASE II

PHASE II

Cartersville Tradition

PHASE II

PHASE II

A ceramic tradition is what archaeologists normally refer to as an **archaeological culture**. It is possible to determine the origins of a tradition and trace its spread, given that a sufficient number of sites have been dated from a wide enough area.

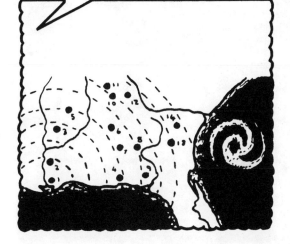

When the dates are plotted against distance, a straight line would be indicative of movement away from a point of origin, either as a diffusion of ideas or a movement of people. Archaeologists know this as a time-space cone.

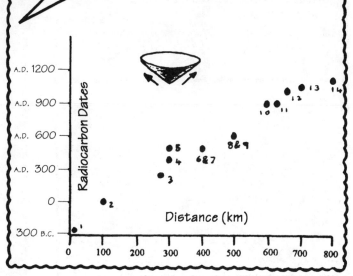

Archaeological cultures are etic devices established by researchers and may or may not correspond to actual linguistic or ethnic groups. Archaeologists must use other methods of investigation, such as oral traditions, settlement layout, and diet, to confirm that. And this still may not correspond to how the original inhabitants viewed the relationships among themselves and with their neighbors.

But it is not only human-made tools that give us information about ancient peoples. Evidence for the consumption and general use of plants comes from plant fragments that have survived in the soils of a site. At the site, soil from excavated features and comparative samples are collected in 10-liter cloth bags. These are taken to a spot on the site for flotation.

Soil from a bag is emptied in the flotation barrel. The agitated water in the barrel separates materials of different specific gravity. The light **fraction**, such as seeds and charcoal, floats to the surface, whereas the heavy fraction, such as nutshell, sinks to the bottom.

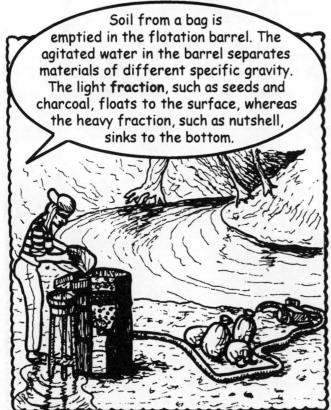

The light fraction is skimmed off the surface or falls into a screen. The heavy fraction is caught in a nylon screen within the tank.

In addition to nutshell, heavy fractions may include small stones, ceramic fragments, and tiny bones. Once separated, the heavy and light fractions are placed on towels to dry and then placed in labeled bags for shipment to the laboratory.

In the laboratory Squizee first pours the light fraction material through nested geologic screens, ranging in mesh size from 0.21 mm to 6.35 mm. Materials smaller than 0.71 mm are mainly fine silt that is normally discarded. Squizee then hands the size-graded light fractions to Ed Dibble, the project's archaeobotanical specialist.

Ed further sorts the illuminated light fractions under a low-power binocular microscope and sorts them with a fine paintbrush. Archaeobotanists mainly concentrate on the surface characteristics of macrobotanical remains for identification purposes.

With the help of a good comparative collection of known modern-day wood, even novices like Squizee can separate charred hardwoods from softwoods within an archaeological collection.

With more experience, different species of carbonized seeds and grains can be identified. An increase in seed size is often indicative of plant domestication. Seeds of wild and domesticated sunflower, or *Helianthus*, can be separated in this fashion.

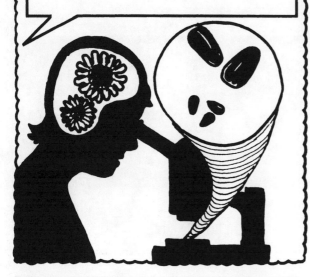

Some changes from wild to domesticated seeds are not so obvious and can only be detected with the aid of a Scanning Electron Microscope, or SEM. With a SEM, seeds can be magnified 200,000 times.

Electrons are generated from a wire gun within the SEM and focused by magnets onto the seed specimen. The seed, which is coated with an atom-thin layer of gold, deflects the electrons to a detector and television monitor.

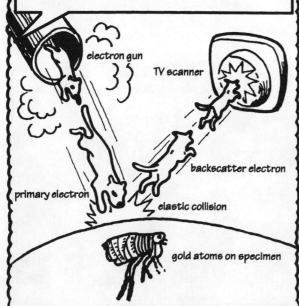

Close-up SEM measurements of the coats of goosefoot, or *chenopod*, reveal a reduction of seed coat thickness among domestic plants. Dates of the oldest chenopod seeds with thin coats suggest that some 3,500 years ago prehistoric Indians domesticated them.

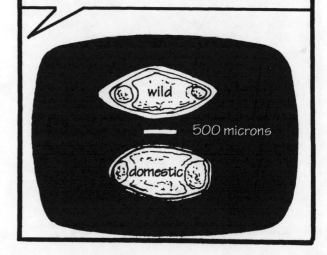

Contemporary evidence suggests that the deliberate sowing of seeds increases plant density. Seedlings with thin coats germinate first and are the most likely to survive in sown fields. Bigger seeds also tend to survive in sown fields since they germinate before smaller ones. Big seeds with thin coats in the archaeological record then strongly suggest deliberate planting.

Wild wheat has stalks that shatter easily and seeds with thick coats. Deliberate harvesting selects wheat with tough stalks and seeds with thin coats. By 8500 B.C. domesticated wheat with tough stalks is known from the Fertile Crescent, an area that includes Iran, Turkey, and Israel, from which the first evidence of plant domestication comes.

Apart from morphological changes in specific plants, indirect evidence for domestication is apparent in the changing relative abundance of different macro-plant remains through time. For instance, an increase in charred pinewood and corncobs relative to acorns might be indicative of field clearing for corn cultivation.

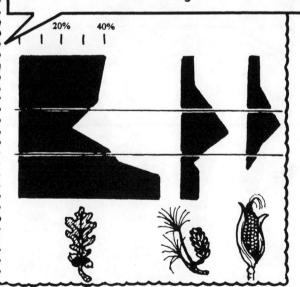

Palynologists study the microscopic grains of plant pollen, or micro-plant remains. Wind-borne pollen has a wide variety of sizes and shapes diagnostic of specific plant species. A relative increase in the pollen of corn and pine versus that of oak could be independent evidence for forest clearing and cultivation.

The counting and interpretation of excavated plant remains is not a straightforward matter; the mere comparison of total counts of different seed species may give a misleading picture of their dietary importance. For instance, the chance discovery of an isolated concentration of otherwise-scarce chenopod seeds at a site may overstate their importance in the overall diet at a site.

Ubiquity counts overcome biases brought about by differential densities and preservation. A ubiquity count of a particular seed species is expressed by the percentage of the total number of occurrences containing seeds. Fifty wild cherry seeds that occur at 4 out of 5 seed occurrences at a site are more ubiquitous than 200 chenopod seeds that are restricted to one occurrence only.

The recovery of wild tobacco seeds and pollen from a hearth in the rock shelter that Ana Lysis excavated stirs some memories for Ed Dibble. Ed knows from ethnographic writings that some Native Americans used tobacco and peyote buttons in their religious rituals.

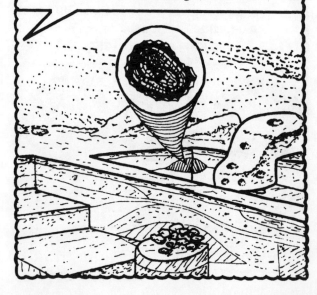

As a student Ed participated in an excavation of a dry rock shelter in the Pecos region on the Texas border where the crew recovered dried peyote buttons. Direct AMS dates of the buttons showed that they were 3,000 years old.

Ed knew that across the border in Mexico the Huichol Indians undertook long pilgrimages to collect peyote buttons, which they ingested to obtain visions and so ensure success in hunting and other pursuits. Huichol shamans sometimes attach peyote buttons to their ceremonial headdresses made of deer antlers.

Rock paintings against the back walls of the Pecos rock shelter that yielded peyote buttons included a depiction of deer antler tines with black dots. These dots have been interpreted as peyote buttons. Direct AMS dates for organic materials within the paint have yielded ages of 3000 B.P.

When Ed "accidentally" ate a piece of peyote, the mescaline molecule within the plant induced him to experience strange visual hallucinations. After this experience Ed the student appreciated the profound affects that altered states have on peoples' views and how these views in turn affected their lifeways.

The various lines of evidence led Ed to agree with archaeologists who proposed a 3,000-year-old peyote-oriented cult in the Pecos region. In this case, plant remains told us about peoples' religious beliefs rather than merely what they ate.

Excavated bone should be treated with the same care as plant remains. Madchen Knochen, the project's zooarchaeologist, is in charge of cleaning, sorting, and identifying the bone remains from 9Go77.

As in the case with the analysis of lithics, ceramics, and plant remains, the identification of bones requires a good comparative collection. This collection should include all ages and both sexes of the animals from the region.

Traditional classification of animals is task specific. In the eighteenth century, Carl Linnaeus grouped species according to physical similarities and inferred evolutionary relationships.

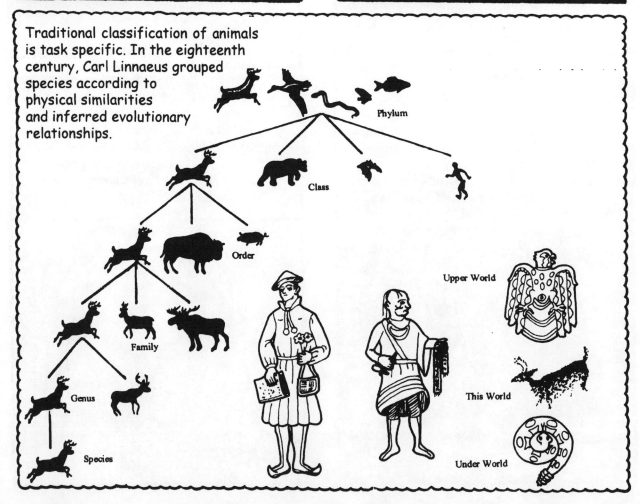

Only a few complete bone fragments can be identified to the species level. By weighing the bones from each species the archaeologist can estimate the amount of meat represented per species. The underlying assumption is that all animals were killed for their meat.

It is important to determine if excavated bones were used by humans. Predators like hyenas, wolves, and lions can also move bones and can leave use marks on them.

A better understanding of bone **taphonomy**, or alteration, can be achieved by background research in the library and in the field.

Madchen's background knowledge of contemporary ethnographic situations gives her a better understanding of bone fragmentation, preservation, and human use.

Not all bone fragments are equally useful in identification. Teeth can typically be linked to specific species. Bone ends are identifiable to side of the body, while shaft fragments are generally unidentifiable.

In order to interpret hunting strategies, it is important to try to identify the age of an animal. Bone ends of juvenile deer have not fused with the main shafts, whereas molar crowns of old deer are worn.

The number of identified specimens, or NISP, is a straightforward list of identifiable animals in an excavated bone collection. The minimum number of individuals, or MNI, is determined by counting the most frequently occurring bone or teeth. The MNI increases if the animals can be distinguished by age.

Lower left first molar

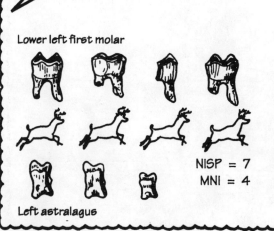

NISP = 7
MNI = 4

Left astralagus

Certain animals have more bones than others and thus might be overrepresented in the archaeological record. Carp have more bones than dogfish, for example.

Carp

Dogfish

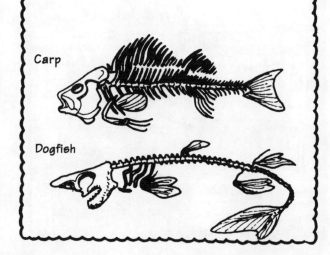

Fragments from widely separated areas may represent different animals, since parts of one animal can be distributed throughout a site. However, scattered bones from the same animal often can help archaeologists understand work relationships between genders, household composition, and other social factors.

Dragging this animal around is a real pain. Sharing with the rest of my band is even a bigger one.

Solid teeth usually last longer than spongy backbones in the archaeological record and are therefore more often found.

However, backbones protected in a trash pit might outlast teeth exposed on the ground surface.

Divergent eating habits should constantly be kept in mind. Brains are desirable food in many cultures. Certain animals are valued for their supernatural powers instead of their meat, while others provide clothing material, ornaments, or tools.

The fact that certain animals are now extinct does not mean we cannot identify them or trace their living descendants . . .

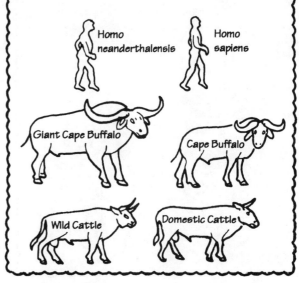

Homo neanderthalensis

Homo sapiens

Giant Cape Buffalo

Cape Buffalo

Wild Cattle

Domestic Cattle

Madchen Knochen examines the human skull that Chief excavated at Ghost Town. A skull contains some clues about the ancestry of that person. The most reliable traits for the determination of ancestry are concentrated in the face and jaw, and, to a lesser extent, in the braincase.

From looking at this skull Madchen can identify some characteristics that are usually associated with African populations, such as the filing of the teeth into an hourglass shape, forward projection of the teeth, flared nasal opening, and elongated cranium.

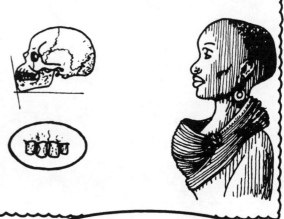

The identification of physical features from skulls is often dismissed as racist. Ironically, it is the identification of Negroid features from skulls associated with stonewalled ruins in South Africa that help convince white supremacist archaeologists that Africans built these settlements.

All these analyses! And they don't all match. How can archaeologists speak so confidently about what happened in the past when they weren't there?

Perhaps you should ask my dad, Abe Strack. He is a professor of philosophy of science at the state university.

CHAPTER 6

SPREADING THE WORD

Sunday night wth the Strack family…

The use of chemical and physical techniques of analysis and dating does not alone make archaeology a science. Archaeology is truly interdisciplinary, but only becomes a coherent discipline within an overall ethnographic framework as a part of the larger field of anthropology.

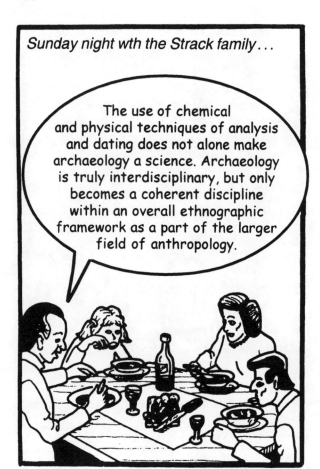

In the longrun all archaeological remains have to be viewed through ethnographic glasses; archaeology is anthropology or it is nothing. To understand the remains of hunter-gatherers, for instance, archaeologists inevitably have to compare them with documented hunting-gathering societies. Archaeologists use their own society as an ethnographic reference point, or analog, when dealing with historic remains.

All archaeologists, even those who claim the contrary, use **ethnographic analogy** to understand the archaeological record. To draw an analogy between the archaeological record and the ethnographic record is to show one or more relevant respects in which they are similar.

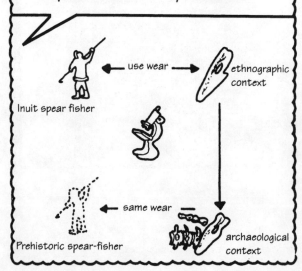

use wear → ethnographic context

Inuit spear fisher

← same wear —

Prehistoric spear-fisher

archaeological context

Archaeological materials do not speak for themselves and can only be understood by reference to known ethnographic processes. For example, those who assume the existence of extraterrestrials have no concrete processes to use as analogs to support their claims about the role of aliens in shaping the archaeological record.

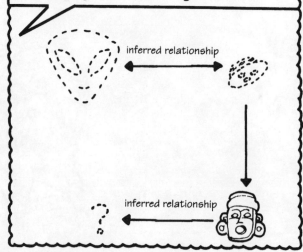

inferred relationship

inferred relationship

Used carelessly, ethnographic analogy can give a misleading picture of the archaeological record. Archaeologists need to be cautious and rigorous when using analogical reasoning. Because analogy is ever present, archaeologists have to constantly wrestle this beast and be careful not to be led by the nose.

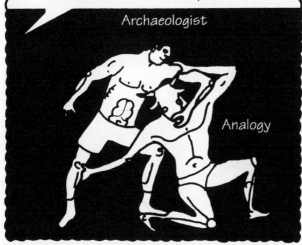

Archaeologist

Analogy

An example of analogy gone astray was when archaeologists interpreted a hunter-gatherer rock painting from southern Africa in terms of ancient Middle Eastern ethnography. The archaeologists interpreted the painting of a female figure surrounded by a group of men as a Mother Goddess and her royal entourage, based upon our knowledge of Mesopotamian mythology.

However, looking at the ethnography of the San hunter-gatherers who are direct descendants of the painters, it becomes clear that they do not have a Mother Goddess in their religious tradition. Instead, San ethnography suggests that the painted panel depicts a shaman's journey to the spirit world.

Ideally then, archaeologists can do well by working from a known ethnographic society in a step-like fashion back into the past. This strategy is known as the **direct historical method**. Direct historical analogy normally illuminates archaeological remains to a degree not possible by more distant analogies.

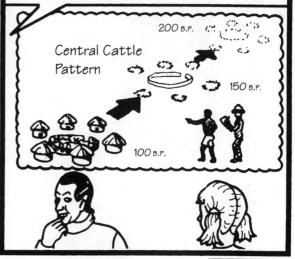

Central Cattle Pattern

200 B.P.

150 B.P.

100 B.P.

Archaeologists can benefit from looking beyond material remains to their place within particular socioeconomic and belief systems. The direct historic approach makes it clear that society and ideology, rather than ecology, ultimately shape the archaeological record.

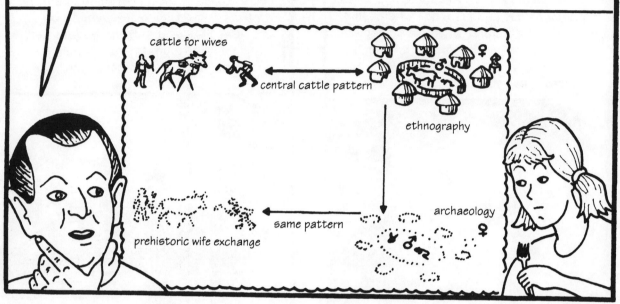

A point is reached when the ethnographic details do not perfectly fit the archaeological record any more. This disjunction is indicative of significant change. Elaborate 800-year-old stone walled ruins in southern Africa, called zimbabwes, indicate the existence of more stratified societies than apparent in the ethnographic record of that region.

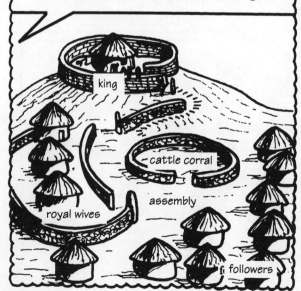

The 1,500-year-old walls in the American Midwest have no apparent analogy among historic period Native American societies in the region. So early western visitors attributed them to everyone from the Romans to the lost tribes of Israel. Modern archaeologists have looked elsewhere to find an ethnographic match, in this case New Guinea.

This match does not mean that the people from New Guinea and North America had past contacts, but rather that the working of their social and economic systems is broadly similar. Such similarities between societies separated by space and/or time allow ethnographers and archaeologists to make comparisons.

Although a wide variety of societies have existed in the world, there are limits to their diversity. Worldwide similarities in the functioning of the brain account for the finite set of past technologies and kinship systems, for example.

The three-tiered hierarchy of settlement size from 1,500-year-old sites in the American Midwest corresponds to the hierarchy found in New Guinea. This **site hierarchy** is indicative of social hierarchy.

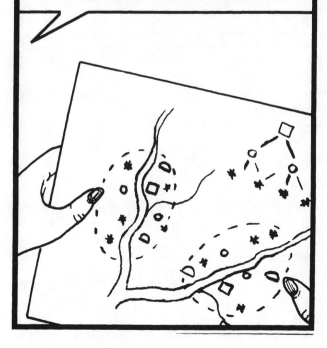

As in the case of New Guinea, scarce goods that have been traded over long distances ended up in the burials of certain individuals in the American Midwest. The accumulation of **prestige goods** and settlement hierarchy are indicative of economic systems controlled by **"big men"** or **"big women."** Our simple term for them is **chiefdom**.

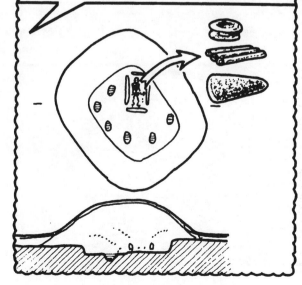

Seasonally occupied camps characterize the many societies based on **communal production** and reciprocal exchange. At some times of the year, the groups aggregate together; at other times, they are dispersed into smaller **bands**. People hunt wild animals and collect wild plants, and have limited storage facilities. Individuals make their own tools; shamans tend to the well-being of the camps.

A hierarchy of semipermanent settlements characterizes societies based on **tributary production** and redistribution. People herd domestic animals and cultivate domestic plants and have bigger storage facilities. Part-time specialists make tools and hereditary chiefs and diviners rule the chiefdom.

A centralized settlement system characterizes societies based on production for long-distance exchange of prestige goods. Full-time specialists make scarce items and slaves mine precious metals. Big containers store the increased output of food. A dynastic class of kings and priests rule the **state**.

These divisions are not so clear-cut in reality. A "big man" system, for example, falls between communal and tributary production. Also, chiefdoms are not always associated with agriculture; the Northwest Coast Indians of North America are stratified hunter-gatherers based on the massive harvesting of wild aquatic animals like fish and whales and wild terrestrial plants.

It was thought that nomadic animal herders, or pastoralists, are always male dominated until . . .

. . . the discovery of female skeletons in pastoralist sites of the Ukraine and Russia buried with mirrors, earrings, beads, and arrowheads. Some skeletons with bowed leg bones and others with arrowheads embedded in their ribs suggest that they were influential warrior women.

The discovery of multiple frog bones in a pit . . .

. . . could be interpreted as evidence of a frog licking cult . . .

. . . but a scenario of frogs killed in a frozen puddle might be more plausible.

One should be cautious not to make up analogies or push them too far. Eighteen-thousand-year-old oval dwellings made of mammoth bone in the Ukraine have no obvious analogies in the ethnographic record. After all, mammoths are extinct. Yet from their good preservation it is possible to reconstruct their original form.

In order to better understand the behavior of early people, dating back almost a million years ago, archaeologists use primates as analogs; assuming that they are closer in time and evolutionary development.

I guess it's getting late . . .

and tomorrow the two of you have to meet with Bianca Cash at the new museum site.

With money provided by the philanthropist Bianca Cash, the Gopher County Trust was formed to oversee construction and subsequent operation of a museum on Squizee's family land.

Skillful popularization provided by this on-site museum would be an effective way for Dr. Holmes and his colleagues to reach the general public with their findings. Dr. Holmes' involvement in all stages of the project would ensure proper interpretation, **presentation**, and **preservation**.

Yes, properly planned displays educate people by placing excavated features and artifacts in context.

I would like to see displays include scale models and life-size reconstructions. In addition, it would be nice if paying visitors can partake in ongoing excavations and laboratory work on the museum grounds. Of course, a museum theater and shop with an archaeological theme would provide educational material and additional income. It is up to Dr. Holmes and his team to develop an interpretive theme and content of displays to match.

I suggest we follow a theme of world prehistory within which we then present the prehistory of Gopher County. World prehistory can be presented in terms of pivotal points; the origins of physically modern people, the first art, colonization of the Americas, the extinction of mega-fauna, the domestication of plants and animals, and the emergence of complex societies.

Squizee and Amitai can help the various specialists interpret the archaeological record for display purposes. Meanwhile let's discuss the museum layout over lunch.

This should be fun!

The origin of physically modern people is a question that goes way back in time and is subject to continual controversy.

Since the nineteenth century, religious fundamentalists have been squaring off with evolutionists over the identity, date, and location of the first people.

A sequence of robust to gracile skulls supports the evolutionary model, while the occurrence of older gracile skulls challenges this interpretation of human evolution.

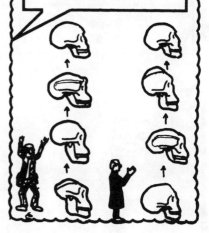

The current collection of skeletal remains from across the world supports the evolutionary model. However, anatomists disagree about the details of evolution, mainly due to incomplete dates for branching but also due to disagreements concerning pertinent anatomical features.

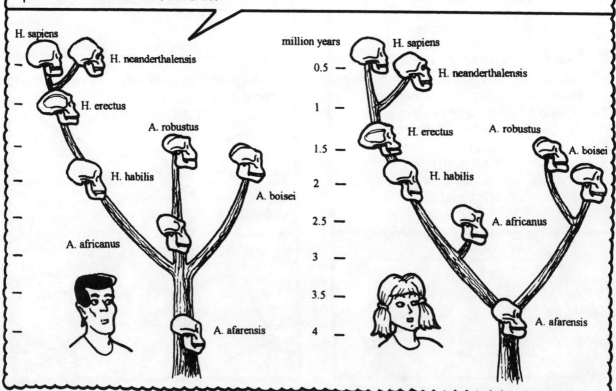

There is general agreement that the first hominids, or human-like beings, lived in Africa. Fossilized Australopithecus bones have been found along the Great Rift Valley of East Africa and the limestone caves of Southern Africa, dating to 3 to 2.5 million years ago. From these evolved *Homo habilis,* the first beings that produced tools, between 2 to 1.5 million years ago.

By 250,000 years ago *Habilis* evolved into Erectus, a tool producing and erect walking being that moved out of Africa into other parts of the "Old World," such as Europe, Asia, and Australia. Between 100,000 and 60,000 years ago, we know that modern *Homo sapiens* were present in Africa. It is still debated whether or not *Homo sapiens* developed separately elsewhere in the "Old World" or whether all migrated out of Africa.

The **Out of Africa Replacement Model** claims that *Homo sapiens* from Africa replaced more archaic populations elsewhere in the "Old World" without admixture.

Support for the Out of Africa model would be evidence that *Homo sapiens* replaced *Homo neanderthalensis* in Europe with no interbreeding between the two populations.

The **Multiregional Local Development Model** claims that some *Homo sapiens* evolved independently out of archaic populations in Asia and Australia.

Support for the multiregional model would be evidence of interbreeding in each region, such as between *Homo sapiens* and *Homo neanderthalensis.*

She supports separate development.

Ana Lysis is in charge of the rock art exhibit.

He supports racial distinction.

Amitai is holding a bone carved by a Neanderthal and Squizee a statuette carved by a *sapiens*.

The realism of the oldest art has surprised archaeologists and art historians. The 31,000-year-old rock art in the Chauvet Cave of southern France includes lifelike representations of rhinos, lions, and mammoths.

Most scholars agree with evidence that *Homo sapiens* created this art, but there is disagreement on the reasons why. An early school proposed that the rock art is art-for-art's sake, or for aesthetic expression. This explanation does not account for the selectivity of subject matter or the occurrence of abstract signs, however.

Another school maintains that the art was done as hunting magic, to ensure success in hunting. Proponents of this school refer to some Australian rock art that Aborigines paint to ensure reproduction of natural animal species. Unfortunately, most of the species depicted in the French caves are not turning up as bones in the trash dumps created by these early humans.

A more recent school maintains that ethnographically documented rock art in North and South America and South Africa suggests that shamans created the earliest European rock art. Proponents of this school cite as support the unusual abstract elements in the designs, the incorporation of the natural surfaces of the rock in the art, and the fusion of humans and animals.

It's all aesthetics.

Sympathetic magic makes more sense.

But it might yet be the most bizarre explanation—shamanic.

Shamans are important in virtually every hunting and gathering society. Almost invariably these people experience vivid visual hallucinations that they believe help them to cure people, influence the weather, and control the movements of animals.

We know that in moments of reflective tranquility shamans often paint or engrave the visions they had in trances or dreams. Neuro-mathematicians have shown that the geometric forms seen by people in altered states have their origins in the visual cortex of the brain. The neurologically controlled imagery might then account for the worldwide occurrence of certain abstract images in rock art.

People in deep trance sometimes see themselves turning into animals. The portrayal of half-animal creatures, or **thereanthropes,** in the earliest rock art from Europe and Africa might be a depiction of the altered-state fusion of person and animal.

Particular similarities in the shamanic practices among cultures from the polar regions of Asia and North America have led some ethnographers to propose ancient physical contacts between people from these regions.

Physical similarities between people from Asia and North America, including regionally exclusive teeth traits, known as **sinodont,** seemingly support proposed population links. Similarities in certain stone tool forms on both sides of the Bering Straits do not contradict this scenario.

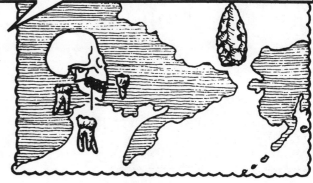

These beautifully fluted Clovis points were made more than 11,000 years ago in much of North America by Paleoindian hunters thought to be descendants of the first migrants to cross the Bering Straits some 12,000 years ago.

Toward the end of the last Ice Age, or Pleistocene, lowered ocean water locked up in massive ice sheets left a land bridge across the Bering Straits. Some archaeologists believe that people crossed this bridge and reached the rest of North America through a gap in the ice sheets no earlier than 12,000 years ago.

But discoveries of earlier sites in South America have upset the Clovis scenario. Convincing evidence from the Monte Verde site in Chile shows that pre-Clovis artifacts there are at least 12,500 years old.

Monte Verde

The discovery of pre-Clovis sites that far south has led archaeologists to propose more direct alternative migration routes, one being along the west coast of North America.

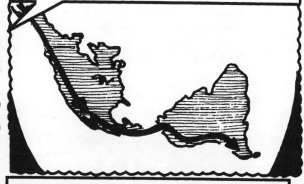

A 9,000-year-old skull discovered next to the Columbia River near Kennewick, Washington, has complicated the picture. Some archaeologists feel that this skull exhibits European, rather than East Asian, characteristics. Stone tools from even earlier sites on the east coast show similarities to Solutrean points in Europe. Most archaeologists still view these interpretations with skepticism.

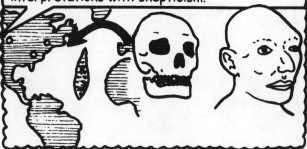

Such anomalous findings that challenge conventional interpretations must stand up to intense scrutiny before they are accepted by the archaeological community.

I think the European connection should be explored further.

Why are you so obsessed with Europe and Europeans?

Never mind, apart from feuding archaeologists . . .

. . . I have to contend with fundamentalists, both from Native American and European camps. Native American myths insist that they always lived in North America, contrary to what archaeologists think. Some clergy maintain that the great flood of Noah wiped out all evidence of the past only a few thousand years ago.

Some creationist supporters of an antediluvian scenario believe that the animals that are not with us anymore probably died during a biblical flood. Based on archaeological evidence, however, a wave of animals became extinct between 50,000 and 11,000 years ago, a span of 40,000 years. In North America most of these extinctions occurred near the end of the last glacial age, some 13,000 to 11,000 years ago.

Two main explanations have been proposed for the mass disappearance; the **overkill hypothesis** and the **climatic change hypothesis**. The overkill hypothesis maintains that, once hunters became organizationally and technologically proficient with weapons tipped with Clovis points, they started to successfully hunt larger animals and so cause their demise.

Supporters of the climatic change hypothesis propose that changes from steppe to woodlands, greater temperature extremes, drier conditions, and disrupted birth scheduling caused mass extinctions of large animals—**megafauna**—at the end of the Ice Age.

But in Africa and Australia extinctions of some megafauna occurred prior to the end of the Ice Age, so climatic change alone cannot be held responsible. We know from positive archaeological evidence, such as stone projectile points in carcasses and butcher marks on bone, that big animals were hunted.

I think environment does play an important role!

You are taking agency away from people!

What's up with those two?

Just a normal discussion between archaeologists.

The next big event in prehistory is the **domestication**, or genetic alteration, of plants and animals. There is a difference between the intensive use of a resource, such as a hickory tree, and the production and genetic change of that resource, such as from wild teosinte to domestic maize.

There is also a difference between a tame animal, such as a circus monkey, and a genetically changed animal, such as from wild wolf to domestic dog. Certain plants and animals are more easily domesticated than others.

Highly productive plants that can pollinate themselves in big stands are fairly easy to domesticate. Animals that live in hierarchical groups are also comparatively easy to domesticate.

Wheat and cattle were first domesticated in the Near East some 10,000 years ago. Independent domestication includes sorghum in Niger, sorghum and cotton in China, gourds and corn in Mexico, sunflowers in the southeastern U.S., and peanuts, corn, and cotton in Peru.

Although the spread of domestic plants and animals was rapid in certain areas, we know that many communities resisted domestication because of increased labor required, reduction in diet diversity, reduced mobility, and more disease.

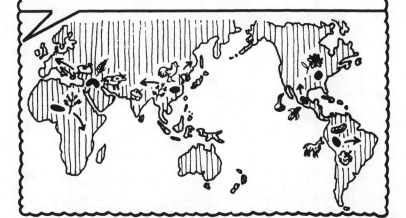

The question of why hunter-gatherers began to cultivate plants and raise animals is not easy to answer. One school proposes that drier conditions after the Ice Age caused people to group together and become sedentary. Living together in bigger settlements increased population size and so forced the inhabitants to more intensively use certain resources. Selection of those resources resulted in their domestication. A social hierarchy developed to control bigger groups of people and the redistribution of resources.

Another school states that plants and animals, such as cotton and llamas, were prestige items rather than food. Prestige goods and food were often involved in payments to prominent individuals. To counteract the onset of drier conditions but yet make their payments, people selected prestigious plants and animals, resulting in their domestication. To properly tend plants and animals people aggregated in bigger settlements. Sedentary living and increased production output resulted in population growth.

These competing views can be tested against the empirical evidence gathered by archaeologists in various parts of the world. But the evidence is usually subject to multiple interpretations. In archaeology there is an ongoing debate between those that give primacy to environmental and technological factors and those that emphasize society and ideology.

Environmental and technical events leave physical evidence for us to study.

Remember, we cannot see atmospheric pressure or property, yet weather and wealth have been crucial in forming the archaeological record.

Social systems and worldviews also leave tangible evidence.

One way out of the environment-versus-society conundrum is to study the two as separate but interacting systems. The level of technology depends on social relations. Ideology is the lubricant that keeps society running. With the separation of society into distinctive classes, the upper class controls ideology. With the advent of industrial society, the upper class possesses technology. Environmental degradation becomes more severe with the development of technology.

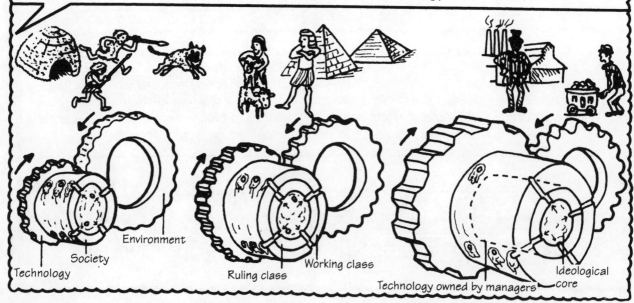

Technology   Society   Environment   Ruling class   Working class   Technology owned by managers   Ideological core

I guess you now realize all the work required to develop museum exhibits. I believe interpretations should give a balanced perspective, based on available evidence. However, interpretation and presentation ought to challenge visitors' preconceptions and so sharpen their critical thinking skills. One way or the other, it is important for archaeologists to share their findings with a broader public. Why don't you two go and look at the completed exhibits in the museum and tell us what you think?

Traditional museum exhibits consist of real artifacts placed within glass display cases. Each case has basic information on the identity, location, and age of the artifacts. Descriptive texts should be short and to the point. Research shows that the average visitor stays at an exhibit case no more than 3 seconds. Maps and interpretive graphics at the back of the case provide further context to the display.

When planning and designing exhibits it is important to have a theme and to order the exhibits within that theme. Exhibits should be ordered in such a fashion so that when visitors walk through a museum the theme unfolds itself. Like cells within a comic, it helps if exhibits make sense in terms of neighboring ones. In this museum, the artifact display leads up to preserved postholes from the excavation.

A reconstructed structure is spatially separated from the real posthole features on which the reconstruction is based. This juxtaposition of excavation and reconstruction in the same exhibit hall not only respects the integrity of the original site 9Go77, but also affords visitors the opportunity to personally evaluate the reconstruction.

Life-size models of the inhabitants give the visitor some impression of what the people might have looked like and how they possibly interacted. The use of natural construction materials, such as wooden posts, thatched roof, and clay floor, imparts the look, feel, and smell from the time period. Recordings of the music and language of historic period Indian groups in the area further adds to the atmosphere.

The museum tour ends in a shop filled with replica artifacts, games, and books of archaeological relevance.

Demonstrations of the production of prehistoric artifacts, like flint knapping or basket making, teach visitors and involve them in motor skills and physical activities. Personal hands-on involvement in artifact reproduction not only gives the participant a better appreciation of nonindustrial technology but also a better grasp of the physical properties of the materials used.

To qualify for official accreditation, the museum has to meet certain minimum standards of curation and conservation. Temperature and humidity levels should be constant and pests should be controlled, for example. Storage facilities should be sufficient to preserve those artifacts not on display and make them easily accessible to researchers. Proper records of the artifact collection and the archaeological work that produced them should be kept and updated on an electronic database as well as on hard paper copies.

The next week, Chief and the crew are jetting to the annual national archaeology conference. Conferences allow archaeologists to talk about their most current research and network with colleagues.

What worries Chief is that he needs a dry run to time his talk on the archaeology of Ghost Town so that it fits the allotted 15-minute slot. It's an important story, showing how archaeology can supplement, and sometimes contradict, the historical narrative as told by archival documents.

The crew is looking forward to the socializing and sightseeing . . .

except for Chief, who has not properly prepared for his lecture.

Squizee and Amitai plan to sightsee and shop between conference sessions . . .

Chief has found an alternative venue to practice for his forthcoming talk and finds a "willing" audience.

Excavations, combined with oral and written history, provided a rare glimpse of Ghost Town, a once thriving community in the Southeast dating between 1780 and 1855. Tobacco exports launched the short but busy life of Ghost Town. Its location on a big river made Ghost Town a most suitable location to load tobacco onto shallow vessels for transport downstream. With the advent of railroads and emergence of cotton, river transport and tobacco diminished in importance.

Cotton and railroads meant the death of Ghost Town. Roughly during this period a handful of free African Americans found refuge in towns, such as Ghost Town, working as manual laborers. This much we can tell from the oral and written record.

Excavated material remains, such as this clay tobacco pipe, fill in the gaps not mentioned in oral or written history. The recovery of this pipe from an African American house is remarkable considering that we found record of a Ghost Town ordinance that forbade African Americans from smoking.

Commie!

Smoking carried cultural meaning among black and white people, since it was a measure of social rank. The recovery of a tobacco pipe from a black house can thus be considered as an act of defiance against the established order in Ghost Town prior to the Civil War.

Meanwhile, 2,600 miles away in Gopher County . . .

THE STRUGGLE CONTINUES . . .

FOR FURTHER READING

Instead of being a comprehensive bibliography, the following list mentions the books, chapters, and articles I found particularly useful while writing the comic. For more detailed bibliographies I recommend readers consult the references quoted in the works listed below.

Aitken, M. J.
 1990 *Science-based Dating in Archaeology*. Longman, London.

Bender, B.
 1978 Gatherer-Hunter to Farmer: A Social Perspective. *World Archaeology* 10:204–222.

Bense, J. A.
 1994 *Archaeology of the Southeastern United States: Paleoindian to World War I*. Academic Press, San Diego.

Binford, S. R., and L. R. Binford
 1972 *New Perspectives in Archaeology*. Aldine, Chicago.

Bowman, S.
 1990 *Radiocarbon Dating*. University of California Press, Berkeley and Los Angeles.

Boyd, C. E., and J. P. Dering
 1996 Medicinal and Hallucinogenic Plants Identified in the Sediments and Pictographs of the Lower Pecos, Texas Archaic. *Antiquity* 70:256–275.

Brothwell, D. R., and E. S. Higgs (editors)
 1969 *Science in Archaeology*. Thames and Hudson, London.

Butzer, K. W.
 1971 *Environment and Archaeology*. Aldine, Chicago.

Conyers, L. B., and D. Goodman
 1997 *Ground-Penetrating Radar: An Introduction for Archaeologists*. AltaMira Press, Walnut Creek.

Copi, I. M.
 1972 *Introduction to Logic*. The Macmillan Company, London.

Cronyn, J. M.
 1989 *Elements of Archaeological Conservation*. Longman, London.

Deacon, H. J., and J. Deacon
 1999 *Human Beginnings in South Africa: Uncovering the Secrets of the Stone Age*. AltaMira Press, Walnut Creek.

Deetz, J.
    1967   *Invitation to Archaeology.* The Natural History Press, New York.

Diamond, J.
    1999   *Guns, Germs, and Steel: The Fates of Human Societies.* W.W. Norton and Company, New York.

Dunnell, R. C.
    1978   *Systematics in Prehistory.* The Free Press, New York.

Fagan, B.
    1986   *People of the Earth: An Introduction to World Prehistory.* Little, Brown, and Company, Boston.

Flannery, K. V. (editor)
    1976   *The Early Mesoamerican Village.* Academic Press, New York.

Friedman, J., and M. J. Rowlands (editors)
    1977   *The Evolution of Social Systems.* Gerald Duckworth, London.

Greene, K.
    1993   *Archaeology: An Introduction.* University of Pennsylvania Press, Philadelphia.

Harris, E.
    1989   *Principles of Archaeological Stratigraphy.* Academic Press, New York.

Haselgrove, C., M. Millet, and I. Smith (editors)
    1985   *Archaeology from the Ploughsoil.* Department of Archaeology, Sheffield.

Hester, T. N., H. J. Shafer, and R. F. Heizer
    1987   *Field Methods in Archaeology.* Mayfield, Palo Alto.

Huffman, T. N.
    1996   *Snakes and Birds: Power and Symbolism in Ancient Zimbabwe.* Witwatersrand University Press, Johannesburg.

Keeley, L. H.
    1980   *Experimental Determination of Stone Tool Uses. A Microwear Analysis.* University of Chicago Press, Chicago.

Klein, R. G., and K. Cruz-Uribe
    1984   *The Analysis of Animal Bones from Archaeological Sites.* University of Chicago Press, Chicago.

Lewis-Williams, J. D.
    1991   Wrestling with Analogy: A Methodological Dilemma in Upper Paleolithic Art Research. *Proceedings of the Prehistoric Society,* 57 Pt. 1:149–160.

McBryde, I. (editor)
    1985   *Who Owns the Past?* Oxford University Press, Melbourne.

McIntosh, J.
    1986   *The Practical Archaeologist: How We Know what We Know About the Past.* The Paul Press, London.

Muckelroy, K.
    1978   *Maritime Archaeology.* Cambridge University Press, Cambridge.

Mueller, J. W. (editor)
    1975   *Sampling in Archaeology.* University of Arizona Press, Tucson.

Oakley, K. P.
    1975   *Man the Toolmaker.* Trustees of the British Museum, London.

Orser, C. E. (editor)
    1996   *Images of the Recent Past: Readings in Historical Archaeology*. AltaMira Press, Walnut Creek.

Orton, C.
    1980   *Mathematics in Archaeology*. Collins, London.

Pearsall, D.
    1989   *Paleoethnobotany: A Handbook of Procedures*. Academic Press, San Diego.

Poirier, F. E.
    1981   *In Search of Ourselves: An Introduction to Physical Anthropology*. Burgess Publishing Company, Minneapolis.

Price, N. S. (editor)
    2001   *The Archaeology of Shamanism*. Routledge, London.

Renfrew, C., and P. Bahn
    1991   *Archaeology: Theories, Methods, and Practice*. Thames and Hudson, London.

Schiffer, M. B.
    1985   *Formation Processes of the Archaeological Record*. University of New Mexico Press, Albuquerque.

Shanks, M., and C. Tilley
    1987   *Social Theory and Archaeology*. Cambridge University Press, Cambridge.

Shepard, A. O.
    1961   *Ceramics for the Archaeologist*. Carnegie Institution of Washington, Publication 609. Washington, D.C.

Sinopoli, C. M.
    1991   *Approaches to Archaeological Ceramics*. Plenum Press, New York.

Smith, B.
    1992   *Rivers of Change: Essays on Early Agriculture in Eastern North America*. Smithsonian Institution, Washington, D.C.

Steward, J. H.
    1942   The Direct Historical Approach to Archaeology. *American Antiquity* 43:337–344.

Taçon, P. S. C.
    1991   The Power of Stone: Symbolic Aspects of Stone Use and Tool Development in Western Arnhem Land, Australia. *Antiquity* 65:192–207.

Tite, M. S.
    1972   *Methods of Physical Examination in Archaeology*. Seminar Press, London and New York.

Trigger, B. G.
    1989   *A History of Archaeological Thought*. Cambridge University Press, Cambridge.

Ucko, P. J. and G. W. Dimbleby (editors)
    1969   *The Domestication and Exploitation of Plants and Animals*. Gerald Duckworth, London.

Whitley, D. S. (editor)
    2001   *Handbook of Rock Art Research*. AltaMira Press, Walnut Creek.

Willey, G. R., and P. Phillips
    1958   *Method and Theory in American Archaeology*. The University of Chicago Press, Chicago.

GLOSSARY

Accelerator mass spectrometry (AMS) radiocarbon dating—This radiocarbon dating technique uses a nuclear accelerator to directly measure the amount of radioactive carbon (^{14}C) atoms in materials that contain organic remains. The direct dating of an artifact is preferable to indirect dating, such as the radiometric radiocarbon dating of charcoal, since it involves no assumptions whether the dated charcoal is indeed contemporaneous to associated undated artifacts. Minuscule contamination, both within the sample and within the accelerator, might skew AMS results, however.

Analogy—An inference based on similarities between two or more phenomena, holding that if these phenomena are alike in respect with certain attributes, then they are also alike in others. Caution should be used when using analogy, bearing in mind that analogical reasoning is likely to yield false conclusions from true premises. An analogy based on relevant, or causative, mechanisms tends to more reliable and successful than those that only consider superficial correspondences.

Archaeological culture—Archaeologists group together diagnostic, or identifiable, artifacts from the same area and time period that look the same, such as long-necked pots with red paint and small arrowheads with serrated edges, into an archaeological culture. An archaeological culture may or may not reflect an actual cultural group, in which people speak the same language and adopt the same customs. The linking of an archaeological culture with an actual group of people needs additional evidence, such as settlement layout and skeletal identification.

Artifact type—This concept refers to a group, or class, of artifacts that share two or more attributes. As no two artifacts are identical and it would be cumbersome, if not impossible, to compare every attribute of an artifact, archaeologists have to choose relevant attributes to define and compare types. Because types are based on general similarities between selected attributes instead of on a virtually infinite number of identical attributes, types are generalized and arbitrary categories assigned instead of all-embracing and natural categories.

Assemblage—An assemblage refers to a group of contemporary and similar artifact types that occur together within a particular site (i.e., they belong to the same component). An assemblage differs from a mere collection of artifacts from a site, in that a collection contains a mixture of artifact types, or multiple components, that might date to different periods and/or belong to different archaeological cultures.

Association—A term that refers to the co-occurrence of artifacts or features with other archaeological remains from the same layer or time period. There are various degrees of association in the archaeological record, not all of equal reliability. A reliable association is where well preserved artifacts are found sealed together in a pit-like feature. A dubious association is where weathered artifacts are scattered throughout a thick soil layer.

Atom bomb effect—The testing of nuclear weapons in the 1950s and 1960s has produced a large amount of excess radioactive carbon (^{14}C) in the atmosphere. The subsequent banning of atmospheric testing resulted in the gradual decrease of excess ^{14}C through the carbon exchange cycle. An unintended result of this episode of nuclear testing and banning was that it allowed nuclear scientists to demonstrate equilibrium in the production, exchange, and uptake of carbon.

Attribute—A minimal characteristic of an artifact used as a basis for classification, or typology. Ceramic attributes commonly include shape, decoration and placement of decoration, color, and raw material. Specifically recurring chemical signatures and/or physical properties of the clay in pots, derived from scientific analyses in a laboratory, can also be regarded as attributes.

Band—Also known as a camp, a band is a small-scale social grouping of gatherers and hunters, generally less than 100 people. Bands move seasonally to exploit wild plants and animals, joining other bands at aggregation sites at least once a year. Inter-band ties and reciprocal sharing play an important part in the lives of these people, as well as frequent appeals to the spirit world for personal supernatural assistance. Bandleaders and ritual specialists tend not to inherit their positions. Band territories are ill defined.

Battleship curves—These are graph-like depictions of the relative frequencies of attributes or types over time. Since the rise, peak, and fall in popularity of artifact types tend to produce battleship-shaped curves, archaeologists sometimes infer time differences from the curves. This technique of relative dating is known as frequency seriation. Unless supported by actual stratigraphic sequences or some other independent means of dating, frequency seriation should be interpreted with caution.

Baulk—In order to preserve physical evidence of the vertical layers within an extensive horizontal excavation, archaeologists sometimes leave narrow strips, or baulks, within an excavated area. A baulk gives good vertical control during excavation and recording, bearing testimony to the different layers within a site that has complicated stratigraphy. Opponents that claim baulks waste time and obscure horizontal patterning of artifacts and features advocate open area excavations—uncovering a site layer by layer.

Big man—This is an anthropological term given to prominent individuals in Melanesia (a group of islands in and around New Guinea of the western Pacific Ocean) who have achieved status through an accumulation of wealth (scarce trade items) and through acumen in religious ceremonies. The position of a big man is not inherited but achieved through control over the production, accumulation, and dissemination of prestige goods.

Calendar dates—A calendar is a system of organizing units of time over extended periods. Various calendars have been used by different cultures in the world. Western historians commonly refer to dates within the Gregorian calendar, which is based on the number of days it takes the earth to revolve around the sun. Even though calendar dates are expressed as B.C. (Before Christ) and A.D. (Anni Domini), these dates do in fact not use the year of Christ's birth as reference, bearing in mind the sketchy historical evidence for the exact year of this event. Some scholars accordingly prefer to use the abbreviations B.C.E. (Before Common Era) and C.E. (Common Era).

Calibrated dates—Due to past fluctuations in the atmospheric content of radioactive carbon (^{14}C), raw counts of ^{14}C in any given sample might be too old or too young, depending on the original amount of ^{14}C in the atmosphere. To bring radiocarbon years in line with calendar years, it is necessary to correct the raw laboratory counts of radioactive ^{14}C against dated tree-rings. Since certain tree species produce a new growth ring per year, radiocarbon dates of the actual rings show the deviation of the radiocarbon date from the tree-ring, or calendar dates. Calibrated dates are not calendar dates for a variety of reasons, the counting error and the uneven calibration curve being two of the most important.

Cartesian grid—By placing an imaginary Cartesian grid over an area of study, archaeologists are able to plot artifacts, cultural features, soil types, and landscape features in terms of x, y (horizontal distances), and z (vertical distance) co-ordinates. By combining coordinate information on artifact counts, feature types, depth below surface, and topography, archaeologists can generate maps that graphically show artifact densities and other patterns.

Chert—A dense, glass-like, and fairly hard rock composed of microcrystalline silica. Chert is most commonly formed when silica replaces limestone. Commonly found in the Southeastern United States, this sedimentary rock may contain pieces of microscopic fossils. Due to its good flaking and cutting properties, chert was often used for making tools. These properties can be enhanced by heating chert over a hot fire, typically turning the rock red and giving it a shiny surface appearance.

Chiefdom—Also known as a tribe, this is a medium-scale social grouping, consisting of at least 1,000 people who are ruled by a hereditary chief and a series of lower ranking headmen. Chiefdoms occur mostly among agricultural or pastoral societies but are occasionally found among gatherers and hunters in areas with abundant resources. Ancestor veneration and lineage-based kinship ties play an important part in the lives of these people, who tend to inhabit semipermanent settlements where they pay tribute to their leaders with food and services. Chiefs redistribute food during annual ceremonies or in times of need. The boundaries between chiefdoms tend to be better defined than band territories.

Choropleth—A geographical term that derives from the Greek words choros (place) and pleth (value). It refers to statistical maps that match distinctive color or shading representing data, such as numbers or ratios of artifacts. The choropleth technique helps the map-reader see spatial qualities and variations in the data and is an appropriate tool for creating a sense of an overall spatial pattern. The technique assumes that the value in the enumeration unit is spread uniformly within the unit.

Classification—The ordering of phenomena into groups, classes, or types on the basis of shared characteristics, or attributes. All classifications are arbitrary in that only certain attributes are used; otherwise every artifact, tree, and bird, would be a unique class. A classification is judged in terms of its purpose; a valid classification is one that eloquently separates artifacts into useful classes. When constructing culture-history sequences, it is useful that artifacts are classed by attributes that best represent groups of people, for example.

Climatic change hypothesis—Certain archaeologists maintain that environmental variables, particularly climate, influence the course of events. Climatic change has been used to explain the extinction of megafauna (giant mammals) towards the end of the last Ice Age, or Pleistocene (between 20,000 and 10,000 years ago). The origins of agriculture are linked to climatic change during the early Holocene (between 10,000 and 8,000 years ago). Whereas archaeologists recognize the constraining effects of climate, many contemporary archaeologists do not view climate as causing change all by itself.

Coil and paddle—A pottery manufacturing technique that involves the use of rolled clay coils to build vessel walls, followed by the welding of the coiled walls with a decorated wooden or ceramic paddle. Parallel breaks between the coils and impressed designs on pottery fragments, or sherds, from the archaeological record are physical evidence of the coil and paddle technique.

Cognitive Archaeology—See Post-Processual School.

Collagen—The protein fraction within bone, comprising various amino acids, which is more suitable for radiocarbon dating than the inorganic calcium-containing component of bone. Unfortunately for dating purposes, bone collagen degrades in heat and can be attacked by bacteria or fungi. Due to degradation and contamination of the carbon within collagen, bone is typically less suitable for radiocarbon dating than wood charcoal.

Communal production—This refers to the cooperative food gathering and raw material collecting and distribution activities among gatherers and hunters and among small-scale agricultural communities. The relationship between producers and consumers is normally based on close kinship ties, and the products of gathering are owned collectively. The remains of butchered wild animals are distributed among the community according to rules of reciprocity.

Component—This is the presence of an artifact type, diagnostic of a particular time period, at a site. A site that only contains diagnostic artifacts from the same time period is known as a single-component site. A site that contains artifacts diagnostic of two or more distinct time periods is known as a multi-component site. All things being equal, single-component sites are usually easier to date and interpret, due to the increased likelihood of disturbance and mixing at multi-component sites.

Consultation—A process where archaeologists communicate with colleagues, the public, and other parties concerned about the site or area under study. By way of this process the archaeologist not only gives other people a better idea of what the project is all about but also gains information on the history, significance, condition, conservation, and interpretation of the site or area. By means of consultation the archaeologist avoids running the risk of doing something that may be incorrect or incompatible with the wishes of other interested parties.

Contexts—The context of an artifact is usually its immediately surrounding matrix (e.g., pit-fill, midden, hut floor, or stone wall), its provenience (i.e., the horizontal and vertical location within the matrix), and its association with other artifacts in the same matrix. The context of an assemblage of roughly contemporary artifacts and features is typically a site or a certain area within a site. The context of a site is the surrounding landforms, vegetation, other natural resources, and neighboring sites. An ethnographic context is the historically documented or living culture known to be associated with the archaeological remains.

Contract firms—These are mostly privately owned and operated businesses that conduct archaeological projects on behalf of clients. Clients are usually agencies or construction companies that have to comply with federal or state legislation concerning the search, location, documentation, identification, interpretation, and conservation of sites and artifacts on land earmarked for alteration. Although contract firms vary in size and organizational set-up, many firms today have a substantial permanent staff on their payroll, complete with benefits and profit sharing. Specialists on the staffs of bigger firms include administrative personnel, principal investigators, field archaeologists, laboratory analysts and conservators, zoo-archaeologists, archaeo-botanists, and graphic artists.

Cross dating—This is the indirect, or external, dating of an artifact and associated site in terms of similarities to artifacts of a known age from a nearby site or group of sites. Cross dating works well as a simple and relative dating method when artifacts from a small area are compared, but becomes less reliable when comparisons are made over long distances.

Cultural formation process—The deliberate and accidental activities of humans that affect the way in which archaeological materials came to be buried and their subsequent history. Discarding trash on a designated pile or into a pit formerly used for cooking are examples of cultural formation processes.

Cultural Resources Management (CRM)—The search, location, documentation, identification, interpretation, conservation, and management of sites and artifacts on land earmarked for alteration or increased use. The CRM industry depends by-and-large on legislation designed to safeguard the past. Archaeological CRM projects typically involve the following three phases: Phase I survey; Phase II testing; and Phase III data recovery. Depending on the outcome of the early phases, a truly intact and/or unique site might be recommended for avoidance instead of being subjected to archaeological excavations or construction.

Culture History—The identification, description, spatial and temporal placement of prehistoric cultures according to diagnostic artifacts and settlement patterns. Adherents of the cultural history school in archaeology use procedures of traditional historians, particularly reconstructing the movements of people in terms of places and dates.

Datum point—A fixed point, natural or arbitrary, chosen and marked by an archaeologist as a reference point to which all measurements on a site are subsequently referred to. Fixed in place and marked in a distinctive fashion, a datum point also helps with the relocation of a site. A datum point is normally the tip of a thin metal rebar that has been inserted deeply into the ground or contained within a concrete block. The height and the horizontal coordinates of a datum point can be established through a global positioning system (GPS) or more precisely through total station measurements of visible trigonomical beacons in the surrounding area.

Debitage—The waste material created by stone tool manufacture is commonly known as debitage. Typical debitage includes flakes, chips, and shatter. Although archaeologists might not necessarily infer the age or function of a site from debitage, the careful excavation and recording of debitage might help archaeologists reconstruct prehistoric lithic reduction activities and raw material procurement locales.

Dendrochronology—Also known as tree-ring dating, the annual variations in climatic conditions that produce differential growth can be used to match and date distinctive tree-rings and to measure environmental change. In the Southwest United States of America detailed work on tree-rings from timber beams and lintels in the stone walls of prehistoric Indian structures has produced one of the most fine-grained chronologies and environmental records in the world.

Diffusionist school—This is a late nineteenth- and early twentieth-century school that focused on the outward spread of attributes, artifacts, and cultures from a few core areas. Maintaining that an invention is most likely made only once, diffusionists study the ways in which the migration of people and/or the spread of ideas contribute to the appearance of new technology and agriculture in different parts of the world. Whereas migrations of people and the spread of ideas undoubtedly occurred in the past, there are instances where inventions were made independently in widely separate parts of the world, such as the bow and arrow, rock art, ceramics, and agriculture. Also, diffusion alone does not explain the process of understanding, accepting, and successfully adopting things that are introduced from the outside.

Direct historical method—An approach drawing relevant analogies between a culture that has been observed and recorded in the historical period and its immediate prehistoric ancestors.

Domestication—This is the process of human control over the reproduction of certain plants and animals that has resulted in the genetic alteration of these species. The complex symbiotic relationship between domesticators and domesticates have resulted in the fact that most domesticated plant and animal species differ morphologically from their wild ancestors. Societies that have domesticated animals and plants also tend to differ from their gathering and hunting predecessors.

Ecological Perspective—Also known as cultural ecology, this approach views culture as the primary adaptive mechanism to the environment. Empirical evidence has shown this to be an over-simplification, since many cultures change or remain static regardless of environmental changes.

Electron Spin Resonance (ESR)—In addition to serving a variety of experimental and analytical purposes in physics, ESR has also been used to measure the trapped electron population that has built up within a sample since its formation, such as within the crystal structure of tooth enamel or sea shell. Nuclear radiation causes the gradual build-up of trapped electrons. The greater the number of trapped electrons that resonate at a particular electromagnetic frequency, the older the sample. A number of problems still accompany this dating technique, such as the unknown history of uranium uptake and continued crystallization after death.

Emic—The makers' and users' classification of things within their own culture, such as a potter's and a client's shared view of a pot's function (derived from the concept of phonemics in linguistics).

Ethnographers—Called Cultural Anthropologists in the United States of America and Social Anthropologists in Britain, these scholars meticulously observe, record, compare, and interpret living communities and/or communities documented in the written historical record.

Ethnographic analogy—This involves the comparison of the archaeological record with ethnographic observations. If used carelessly, this comparison may yield misleading conclusions. At least three different uses of ethnographic analogy can be distinguished in the archaeological literature. First, analogies based on a single resemblance, known as ethnographic precedents, are not very reliable and are best treated as sources for potentially useful ideas. Second, analogies based on multiple correspondences, or parallels, are more reliable but can include irrelevant, or trivial, associations. Third, analogies based on relevant correspondences are most trustworthy since they seek to outline the same causal mechanisms in the archaeological and ethnographic records.

Ethnography—A subdiscipline of anthropology concerned primarily with the nonbiological aspects of historical and contemporary societies and cultures, particularly their behavioral, cognitive, economic, gender, linguistic, political, and technological aspects.

Etic—A classification imposed on things by an outside observer, such as an archaeologist or ethnographer dealing with prehistoric ceramics (derived from the concept of phonetics in linguistics). The systematic and repeatable nature of an etic approach determines its success, instead of its actual reflection of the makers' conceptions.

Evolutionist school—Dating back to the nineteenth century conceptions of biologists and anthropologists, this school emphasizes the processes of independent development and invention in different parts of the world, given that the conditions are roughly similar. Crude evolutionism maintains that societies always develop from simple to complex, depending on environmental pressures. Comparatively subtle multilinear evolutionism takes into account the properties of societies and their response to changing internal conditions, neighboring societies, and environmental constraints. Evolutionism relies heavily on the principle of uniformitarianism, in that causes and effects in the distant past are the same as in the present.

Facie—Culture history term used by certain archaeologists to refer to the geographic, or spatial, extent of similar ceramic assemblages. The term phase refers to the chronological, or time, extent of a particular facie.

Flint—Similar to chert, flint is a dense, glass-like, and fairly hard rock composed of microcrystalline silica. Commonly found in England, flint is most commonly formed when silica replaces chalk.

Fossil fuel effect—Also known as the Suess effect, it was recognized that tree-rings corresponding to the early half of the twentieth century had a significantly lower ^{14}C content than expected, and this was shown to be due to the burning of fuel such as coal. To avoid reference to reduced levels of ^{14}C in the atmosphere, all radiocarbon dates are measured to an oxalic acid standard projected to the year 1950. For this reason radiocarbon dating scientists always refer to 1950 as the present, or zero; raw radiocarbon measurements are quoted as years Before Present (B.P.), or A.D. 1950.

Fractionation—Certain plants tend to take up the lighter carbon isotopes, ^{12}C and ^{13}C, in preference to the heavier ^{14}C. Living plants and animals that eat the plants accordingly tend to have a lower ^{14}C level than the atmosphere. If the difference is significant, the plants and animals will appear older than the atmosphere when dated. This differential uptake, or fractionation, can be checked and corrected by measuring and comparing the concentrations of stable ^{12}C and ^{13}C and then calculating the correct amount of ^{14}C according to shifts in the $^{12}C/^{13}C$ ratio, if any.

Functionalist school—Dating back to the second quarter of the twentieth century, this school emphasizes the need for anthropologists to study the processes that make societies work. Functionalism leads one to think of a society as a living system, the parts of which are related to each other and contribute to the maintenance of that system. Within archaeology functionalism is best expressed through the processual school. Unlike classic functionalist ethnologists, who treat social systems as self-regulatory, processual archaeologists stress the relationship between society and environment as a basis to understand change.

Geomorphology—A subdiscipline of geography and geology, geomorphologists study the form and development of the landscape, including sediments, or soils. Among other information, geomorphologists can advise archaeologists whether sediments are in place, redeposited, created naturally, or are due to the activities of people.

Global Positioning System (GPS)—GPS provides specially coded satellite signals that can be processed in a GPS receiver, enabling the receiving archaeologist to record and later re-locate the location of a site according to UTM coordinates. The UTM, or the Universal Transverse Mercator grid, measures in meters east and north from two perpendicular reference baselines. While there are many thousands of civilian users of GPS worldwide, the system was designed for and is operated by the United States of America's military.

Half-life—At death plants and animals cease to take in ^{14}C from the atmosphere and the concentration of ^{14}C atoms starts to fall, or decay, at an exponential rate. For ^{14}C, exponential decay implies that after 5,730 years, half of the original number of atoms is left in a dead plant or animal.

Harris Diagrams—Designed by Edward Harris to record the complicated stratigraphy of urban archaeological sites, these diagrams are used to represent dispersed three-dimensional layers in a simplified two-dimensional form.

Historical archaeologists—Archaeologists trained to study the material remains of historically documented cultures, principally by comparing these remains with old documents. In Europe historical archaeologists focus on the medieval and post-medieval periods, whereas in the former colonies, such as in Africa, Australia, and the Americas, historical archaeologists research colonial and post-colonial periods.

Hominids—A zoological term referring to humans and their immediate and recognizable ancestors and relatives. Typical characteristics of hominids include enlarged and reorganized brain cases, evidence for upright bipedal locomotion, and small canine teeth associated with molars that have large flat grinding surfaces.

Ideology—In a broad sense this concept refers to the ideas, beliefs, values, and cognitive processes characteristic of a particular group of people, be it an egalitarian hunter-gatherer band or a stratified twenty-first century nation-state. Post-processual archaeologists maintain that knowledge of particular ideological notions, or cosmologies, is crucial to understand social and economic systems and interaction with the environment.

Inclusions—When people collect clay for pottery manufacture, the clay often includes bigger particles, such as sand or tiny stones. Not only is it is difficult and time-consuming to remove all such inclusions from the clay prior to the coiling and shaping of a pot, but sometimes potters wish to leave inclusions in the clay in order to counteract shrinkage or cracking during firing.

In situ—The original placement of an artifact, layer, feature, or structure encountered on the surface or during excavations.

Integrity—Archaeological sites with good integrity are those with comparatively intact layers and features (i.e., well-preserved contexts). Sites with bad integrity are those that have been disturbed by natural and/or human agents. Sites with good integrity, regardless of size or content, are comparatively valuable for research and conservation purposes.

Interpretation—Term used mostly by post-processual archaeologists in reference to our attempt to understand, or derive meaning from, the archaeological record. Unlike the processual school's positivist belief that we can actually reconstruct the prehistoric record, the post-processual school maintains that the best we can do is offer plausible interpretations of the prehistoric past.

Isoline—Like a contour line, this is a line that represents a constant value, such as the same number of artifacts, on a two-dimensional map.

Judgmental surveys—Based on thorough experience of a particular area to be surveyed, archaeologists often focus on particular landforms known to contain sites. The preferred sampling of such high probability landforms is known as judgmental. Whereas judgmental surveys usually produce positive results and save time, opponents have argued that such surveys are self-fulfilling prophecies and might miss important sites.

Knapping—Term used for the flaking and chipping of stone to produce stone tools. Contemporary knappers demonstrate great skill and patience in reproducing the often-intricate stone tools made by prehistoric people.

Layer—Also called a stratum, this term refers to the naturally or culturally created deposit removed during excavation. Ideally, layers are removed and screened as separate "natural" units, but layers normally thicker than 10 centimeters are subdivided into artificial levels.

Level—Also called a spit, this term refers to deposits of arbitrary but consistent thickness removed during excavation. The main purpose of a level is to maintain vertical control over the recovery and recording of artifacts. Depending on the intricacy of the deposits, levels are typically excavated in 5- or 10-centimeter increments.

Linear regression statistics—Positive correlation between two sets of data is seldom perfect in the archaeological record, so the insertion of a line that gives the closest approximation to the relationship between the sets is required. Such a line is known as a regression line. Considering that the visual insertion of a regression line is guesswork, calculation of the "least squares" ensures that the individual observed values from the line are at an absolute minimum.

Locus—This term normally refers to an artifact concentration, or "hot spot," within a site. Bigger sites typically contain several loci. Loci might represent different things, ranging from separate activity areas within the same settlement to distinctive settlements dating to different periods.

Megafauna—Latin for "large animals," this term refers to mammals that became extinct in various parts of the world during the latter part of the last Ice Age, or Pleistocene. In North America extinct megafauna include giant sloths, mammoths, and saber-toothed cats. In Africa, the giant Cape buffalo, giant Cape horse, and giant warthog became extinct. Australian examples include strange animals such as marsupial lions. Explanations for the extinction of these animals vary, ranging from overhunting to changing climatic conditions.

Multi-component sites—Sites that contain artifacts from more than one cultural period or from more than one cultural group. To be truly multi-component, a site needs at least two distinctive assemblages of artifacts, preferably with associated features, instead of only isolated, or "chance," artifacts that could have been brought to the site via trade, collection, or natural redeposition.

Multiregional local development model—In the debate on the origins of modern humans (*Homo sapiens*), proponents of this model cite skeletal evidence that supports Africa, Europe, Asia, and Australia as independent centers of origin. Although supporters of this model may submit that ancient peoples (*Homo erectus*) most likely have their origins in Africa, they argue that once *Homo erectus* groups settled in the new continents these groups separately evolved into modern humans.

National Register of Historic Places (NRHP)—The National Register of Historic Places is the United States of America's official list of cultural resources worthy of preservation. Authorized under the National Historic Preservation Act of 1966, the National Register is part of a national program to coordinate and support public and private efforts to identify, evaluate, and protect archaeological resources.

Native American Graves Protection and Repatriation Act (NAGPRA)—The United States Native American Graves Protection and Repatriation Act of 1990 was established by a congressional vote that removed archaeologists from their conventional role as sole custodians of the archaeological record, shifting this position to concerned Native American groups. This legislation limits what archaeologists can excavate, analyze, curate, and display in museums without due consultation with relevant Native American and Native Hawaiian groups.

Natural formation processes—The natural or environmental events that affected the way in which archaeological materials came to be buried and their subsequent history of preservation and degradation. Water-deposited alluvial soils often bury artifacts and features adjacent to big rivers, whereas water erosion may later destroy the same deposits.

"New" Archaeology—*See* Processual school.

Nomenclature—The technical names, or system of words, used in a particular discipline or subdiscipline, ranging from the language of evolutionary archaeology to the specialized terms used by rock art scholars. This glossary tries to clarify common archaeological nomenclature.

Obsidian—A usually black or banded, hard volcanic glass that displays shiny, curved surfaces when fractured and is formed by rapid cooling of lava. Of all the rock types, obsidian arguably has some of the best flaking properties, often leaving very sharp edges. Prehistoric people used obsidian to make a variety of items, including chipped tools and polished mirrors. High quality obsidian, obtained from near certain volcanoes, was often traded over extensive distances.

Old wood problem—Once laid down, a tree-ring ceases to exchange ^{14}C with the biosphere and so begins the radioactive decay of ^{14}C. This means that the older innermost rings would also be older in radiocarbon years. The heartwood of a 300-year-old oak tree that is cut down to build a canoe, for example, would predate the manufacture and use of the canoe by three centuries. Bearing in mind this Old Wood Problem, it is preferable that archaeologists submit twiggy wood or sapwood for radiocarbon dating, where the age-offset between death and cultural use is less.

Out of Africa Replacement Model—In the debate on the origins of modern humans (*Homo sapiens*), proponents of this model cite skeletal evidence that supports Africa as the center of origin. Dispersal of early modern humans out of the

African center resulted in the replacement or assimilation of earlier archaic peoples (*Homo erectus*) in Europe, Asia, and Australia. This school of thought then proposes that ancestors of humans twice moved out of Africa, first as *Homo erectus* and later as *Homo sapiens*.

Overkill hypothesis—The overkill hypothesis argues that humans were responsible for the Late Pleistocene extinction of megafauna in various parts of the world. According to this hypothesis, Late Ice Age hunters were able to kill large numbers of megafauna in part due to improved technology and/or hunting strategies focusing on pregnant females and younger animals.

Oxidation—In open firing atmospheres with abundant oxygen, carbon present in the pottery vessel body is fully consumed, and the vessel will be light in color. Potters often control the firing atmospheres to obtain the desired color, hardness, porosity, and shrinkage.

Palaeo-anthropologists—Scholars who are trained in anatomy and geology to study early human beings, or hominids, in order to reconstruct past environments and the evolution of people.

Palynologist—Botanist who studies pollen (fine powdery grains produced by seed plants) as an aid to reconstruct past vegetation and climates.

Paste—Clay and other fine-grained particles, excluding inclusions and temper additives, that are the basic substances for making ceramic containers.

Phase—Culture history term used by certain archaeologists to refer to a chronological, or time, segment of similar ceramic assemblages within a broader ceramic tradition. The term facie refers to the spatial extent of a particular phase.

Phase I survey—Section 106 of the National Historic Preservation Act requires that to obtain a federal permit or enter into a contract involving federal moneys or federal land, the lead federal agency might find that an archaeological survey of that land is necessary. The purpose of an archaeological survey is to gain an understanding of what is present within the project area and whether any of the archaeological sites, historic structures or traditional cultural properties (TCPs) may be potentially significant resources. Phase I surveys involve the discovery of sites, determination of their size and depth, and assessment of their integrity and research potential.

Phase II testing—Based on the results of a Phase I survey, archaeologists might recommend Phase II excavations to test the research potential of specific sites that demonstrate good integrity. Phase II excavations can only proceed once the lead agency and the State Historical Preservation Officer (SHPO) accept the archaeologist's recommendations. This phase requires an extra level of effort, such as the excavation of test unit squares and the proper mapping of a site. If the lead agency and SHPO agree with an archaeologist's recommendations that a site is eligible for the National Register of Historic Places (NRHP), then that site is either avoided or earmarked for Phase III data recovery.

Phase III data recovery—Ideally, avoidance is preferable to data recovery for "mitigating the adverse effects," or minimizing the damage, of developments on a site. Often avoidance is impracticable and extensive data recovery excavation is the only alternative to recover research information from a site. Archaeological data recovery means digging large areas by hand or by a combination of hand- and machine-assisted excavation. The final report of the Phase III work is more extensive than the other phases since this report is the only record of the site once it has been destroyed by construction.

Place—Whereas the concept of a site focuses on material remains occurring within a particular space, the concept of a place includes landforms and natural resources in and around the site, such as rivers, hills, and plant and animal species. The indigenous perception of a place normally includes the material and spiritual components of the landscape surrounding a settlement or site.

Post-processual school—Influenced by post-modernist trends in the social anthropology of the 1980s, post-processual archaeologists emphasize that people and their thought patterns, instead of outside environmental pressures, to a very large degree account for the archaeological record. This school comprises several subbranches, including critical theory, cognitive archaeology, and gender archaeology.

Potsherd—A fragment of baked ceramic vessel that has survived destructive postdepositional forces in the archaeological record. Prehistoric and historic peoples often collected and modified sherds for a variety of purposes, including to scrape animal hides, shape disks to spin cotton, or ground into a powder for eating. Archaeologists closely look at sherds to identify archaeological cultures, cross date the associated deposits, reconstruct manufacturing methods, interpret vessel function, and consider world-views from the decorated surfaces.

Prehistoric archaeologists—Scholars trained to locate, identify, analyze, classify, date, and interpret the material remains of cultures that have no writing. These cultures are mostly gathering and hunting bands, but also include pastoralists and agriculturist chiefdoms or states without writing.

Presentation—Also known as the display, or marketing side of archaeology, presentation includes the dissemination of research results to colleagues and the public in terms of published books (like this comic), posters, lectures, hands-on activities, and museum exhibits. Presentation is also vital for preservation. For example, cleverly designed, worded, and placed interpretive pedestals at archaeological sites both educate visitors and create a psychological barrier from sensitive deposits or rock art surfaces.

Preservation—This is the protection of artifacts and sites through activities that minimize chemical and physical deterioration and damage and that prevent loss of informational content. The primary goal of preservation is to prolong the existence of artifacts and sites. Conservation is the profession devoted to the preservation of archaeological remains for the future generations to study and enjoy. Conservation activities include examination, documentation, treatment, and preventative care, supported by research and education.

Pressure flaking—Using the sharp tip of an antler or bone, a knapper exerts pressure on a stone artifact to force away many small, thin flakes, gradually sculpting intricate scraping and/or cutting edges. This method of flake removal differs from striking the stone with a hard object.

Prestige goods—An anthropological term designating a limited range of exchange goods to which a society ascribes high value or status. Prestige goods are normally scarce items, either in nature or deliberately made difficult to obtain when influential individuals control the production, distribution, consumption, and destruction of items.

Primary flake—Also known as a cortical flake, this is a stone flake that has its underside, or dorsal aspect, completely covered with the original cortex, or outer rind, of the parent rock.

Processual school—Also known as "New Archaeology," this approach dates back to the 1960s, when archaeologists called for the explicit formulation of research hypotheses and the ongoing testing of research results. This school comprises several subbranches, including systems theory, environmental archaeology, and evolutionary archaeology.

Provenience—Archaeological term for the location of an artifact or feature within an excavation or a site. For the archaeologist the location of an artifact or feature is as important for interpretation as the actual artifact or feature, since location gives the artifact's and feature's context and overall association with other artifacts, layers, and features.

Public archaeology—In general this term refers to archaeology done with the aid of public funds in the interest of the public. This term also applies to the involvement of non-professional archaeologists in the practice of archaeology, such as volunteers doing hands-on excavations, laboratory work, or the designing of exhibits.

Pythagorean theorem—Almost constantly used by archaeologists to construct the right-angled, or 90 degree, corners of surface grids and excavation blocks, this well-known theorem states that the square of the hypotenuse of a right angle triangle is equal to the sum of the squares of the other two sides.

Quartz—Quartz is a very hard crystalline rock, often found in veins within granite. Common colors are clear or milky white. Quartz, the most common mineral on earth, is comparatively difficult to flake into tools. However, quartz is widely associated with supernatural powers among nonliterate cultures. One reason for this association is the creation of an unusual internal flash of light when quartz is struck or rubbed together. In physics this glow is known as triboluminescence.

Quartzite—In geological layers high heat and pressure introduce silica into the pores between the grains of sandstone and change it into quartzite. Silica cement between the sand grains give quartzite superior flaking properties and harder working surfaces than porous sandstone.

Radiocarbon dating—This is a dating technique that measures the amount of radioactive carbon, or ^{14}C, in an organic sample to determine the approximate date at which the organism died. The basic principle underlying this technique is that the unstable nucleus of a ^{14}C atom decays to nitrogen with an electron, or beta particle, being emitted. The rate of beta particle emission is counted in the radiometric technique. Accelerator Mass Spectrometry is the direct measure of the ratio between unstable ^{14}C atoms and stable ^{12}C atoms.

Radiometric dating—Also known as conventional, or indirect, radiocarbon dating, radiometric dating is the measurement of the rate of emission of beta particles per gram of carbon from the unstable ^{14}C atom. To prevent contamination during measurement, such as nuclear fall-out, a sample of carbon is converted to a gas or a liquid. The electrically charged beta particle produces a flash within the liquid and is counted through a photo-multiplier. Limitations of this technique include long counting time and the need for comparatively big samples.

Random error—Variously known as experimental error, laboratory error, or counting error, random error is the statistical estimation of radioactive decay over a long period of time by the actually measured number over a shorter period and by variable counts, or standard deviation. The ± error quoted with a date implies there is a 68 percent chance that the actual result will lie within one standard deviation of the experimental result. The longer one counts, the smaller, in percentage terms, is the error. Increasing either the size of the sample or the counting time will decrease random error. Random error does not account for contamination or for the possible combination of samples with different ages; random error reflects the precision instead of the accuracy of a measurement.

Reduction—In closed firing atmospheres depleted of oxygen, the baked clay of pots appears dark since the carbon in the vessel body is not lost. Potters often control the firing atmospheres to obtain the desired color, hardness, porosity, and shrinkage.

Residuality—Residuality is a cautionary concept used in dating to describe the incorporation of material of an earlier phase of activity in a later archaeological deposit. Broadly speaking this includes heirlooms and unburied trash. Articulated bones are unlikely to be residual, whereas scattered and weathered items are less reliable dating material.

Sampling—In its most general sense sampling is the idea of using information from a part of something to make inferences about the whole. In an archaeological sense sampling is from an incompletely preserved record; archaeologists are making inferences about a population from a sample of it. Different types of sampling strategies adopted by archaeologists include pragmatic sampling (based on ease of access and previous knowledge) and probabilistic sampling (which includes random, stratified random, or systematic sampling).

Section 106—Section 106 of the National Historic Preservation Act (NHPA) of 1966 is the reason for most of the cultural resource work being conducted in the United States of America today. The purpose of Section 106 is to insure that federal agencies consult with state and local groups before nonrenewable cultural resources, such as archaeological sites and historic structures, are destroyed. The Section 106 process seeks to accommodate preservation concerns at the early stages of project planning. The goal of consultation is to identify sites potentially affected by the undertaking, assess its effects, and seek ways to avoid, minimize, or mitigate any destructive effects on the sites.

Sequence—This is a term referring to the succession of diagnostic artifacts through time. Archaeologists arrange ceramics and lithics, for example, into a chronological sequence according to dating evidence, such as stratified layers or the age of associated charcoal.

Shamans—Also called medicine people, people of high degree, clever people, diviners, or doctors, shamans are religious functionaries that have direct access to the spirit world, achieved through altered states of consciousness, such as trance or dreams. Shamans are mainly found among gathering and hunting societies.

Shovel testing—During surveys of wooded areas or areas with deep soils, archaeologists use round nosed shovels to dig holes in order to recover artifacts buried underneath leaves and soil. On a typical Phase I survey, shovel test pits are dug every 30 meters and the dirt is screened through a quarter inch mesh. Shovel tests are between 30 and 50 centimeters in diameter and extend down to one meter or when sterile subsoil or bedrock is reached. Small sites can be missed by this technique, unless shovel test intervals are narrowed, such as on high probability landforms.

Single-component sites—Sites that contain artifacts from one cultural period or from one cultural group. To be truly single-component, a site needs to have an adequately sampled artifact assemblage, preferably with associated features, instead of isolated, or "chance," artifacts that could have been introduced by natural redeposition or accidental loss.

Sinodont—The term Sinodont refers to people who have Chinese-like teeth. Sinodonts have strong incisor shoveling, single-rooted upper first premolars, and triple-rooted lower first molars. Sinodonts are found in northern Asia and the Americas. Linguistic and genetic evidence tends to support the dental evidence of former movements between Siberia and North America.

Site—An archaeological term for the distinct spatial grouping of artifacts, features, and organic remains that are residues of human activities. A site may represent a single settlement, such as a camp, hamlet, village, or town. Alternatively, a site may comprise overlapping settlements from different periods or annual reoccupations. Juxtaposed sites might have originally been part of one settlement, being divided by an empty communal gathering space, for example.

Site hierarchy—This refers to site size and functional differences within group of roughly contemporary sites. Depending on the artifacts, features, and food remains found within sites, a hierarchy could indicate different economic arrangements, ranging from seasonal movements between an aggregation camp and smaller dispersal sites to a political hierarchy between a central chiefly town and tributary villages. The more elaborate the site hierarchy, the more intricate the economic arrangements.

Standard deviation—This term refers to the probability that the actual age of a dated sample differs from the measured age in the laboratory by a given amount. The ± error quoted with any date implies there is a 68 percent chance that the actual result will lie within one standard deviation from the measured result or a 95 percent chance that it will lie within two standard deviations.

State—A term used to describe a stratified social formation, consisting of at least 10,000 people, who are ruled by a class of nonmanual laborers, including a king and special officials, such as priests, generals, and administrators. States occur mostly among agricultural societies but are occasionally found among pastoralists. State sponsored religion and divine rulers play an important part in the lives of these people, who tend to inhabit permanent settlements and build monumental structures in honor of their rulers. The boundaries between states tend to be well defined and long distance trade in prestige goods is commonplace.

State Historical Preservation Officer (SHPO)—The federally mandated person and office responsible for federal cultural resource compliance at the state level in the United States of America. Every state has one, with a staff that varies in size and specialty. There is usually at least one review archaeologist on the SHPO's staff. The SHPO plays a crucial role mediating between the developer, the federal agency, and the archaeological consultant.

Stratigraphy—Through time the natural accumulation of soil layers or the culturally deposited materials within a site create a succession of layers, or stratigraphy. A succession of layers should provide a relative chronological sequence, with the earliest at the bottom and the latest at the top. Careful study of stratigraphy might also tell how a site was formed.

Superpositioning—This term refers to the direct overlapping of archaeological layers and/or features, with the earliest at the bottom and the latest at the top. Juxtapositioning refers to neighboring layers and/or features.

Systematic Error—The accuracy of laboratory dates are determined by systematic errors, such as faulty equipment. Dating laboratories test whether or not they have systematic errors by comparing their results with those of other laboratories on the same samples.

Temper—Inclusions deliberately added to clays to improve workability and to counteract shrinkage or cracking during firing. Deliberately added material includes crushed stone, sand, crushed shell, crushed pottery, or plant fiber.

Terminus ante quem—Latin for "date before which," this term refers to contexts that pre-date dateable material covering it, such as a rock art motif covered by a layer that has been dated by AMS. However, samples with a substantial age offset, such as massive tree trunks or highly weathered artifacts, do not represent reliable dates for underlying contexts.

Terminus post quem—Latin for "date after which," this term refers to contexts that post-date charcoal or dateable artifacts within. For example, we know that a tree had to die and burn before entering the archaeological record as charcoal, so it will predate the hearth in which it was found. Embossed dates on historic period artifacts similarly predate the brick ruins covering them.

Therianthrope—A being depicted in rock art that combines aspects of two or more species, usually a conflation of a human and an animal.

Thermoluminescence (TL) dating—This technique directly dates archaeological artifacts such as ceramics and burnt flint. Unlike radiocarbon dating, the observed TL signal increases with age. The underlying principle behind TL dating is that the amount of light emitted by the heated sample in the laboratory is proportional to the number of trapped electrons, which in turn is proportional to the amount of nuclear radiation to which the clay particles have been exposed.

Traditional cultural property (TCP)—This term refers to the holy places, ceremonial sites, and other traditionally important places of Native Americans or Native Hawaiians. To be eligible for listing in the National Register of Historic Places (NRHP) a TCP must be a tangible place, be important to native communities today, have integrity, and have some definable boundaries. Under these criteria not all TCPs are eligible for the NRHP; one reason is that native groups sometimes see spatially separated places as interconnected.

Tributary production—This refers to the production of surplus food among agriculturists and affluent gatherers and hunters that are earmarked as payment to a chief. Surplus plant food is normally stored in big containers, such as underground pits. The chief is expected to redistribute food during feasts or in times of need. Among societies with domesticated animals, livestock such as cattle, camels, and horses tend to end up with the ruling families through tributary payments, raiding, and the inflated bride prices demanded for the chiefs' daughters.

Typology—The systematic classification of artifacts into types on the basis of shared attributes considered relevant to a particular study. Instead of being "right" or "wrong," a typology should rather seen as a working system that employs consistent criteria to classify things into useful categories.

Ubiquity—In archaeobotanical studies presence/absence ubiquity ratios of plant species is calculated by dividing the number of proveniences that yielded particular plant species by the total number of proveniences that yielded plant remains. Expressed as percentages, ubiquity is more suitable for comparison than absolute raw counts. One reason is that the percentages are not skewed by the concentration of a particular plant species in any one provenience within a site. Ubiquity percentages are also not influenced by the numbers or proportions of other plants at a site.

Underwater archaeology—Underwater archaeology includes a wide variety of sites, such as springs, submerged lakeside settlements, and marine sites ranging from shipwrecks to drowned cities. With improvements in scuba gear and miniature submarines, the pace and scale of discovery have greatly increased in recent years. The excavation of underwater sites is time consuming and expensive, considering that artifacts have to be carefully excavated, recorded, and conserved, often in difficult conditions.

Uniformitarianism—This is the principle that the same natural and cultural causes and effects have prevailed in all ages; comparisons of observed processes in the present also apply to the remote past. This principle stands in contrast with catastrophism, a religious fundamentalist view that maintains certain catastrophic events in the past have subverted the system of things; secular observations in the present do not account for divinely inspired occurrences in the remote past.

INDEX

ABOUT THE AUTHOR

Johannes Loubser was trained in archaeology at the University of the Witwatersrand in South Africa, where he completed Masters and Ph.D. theses on the ceramics, oral traditions, and the impressive stone-walled towns of the Bantu-speaking communities in the northern part of the country. After studying at the rock art department at the Bloemfontein National Museum in South Africa in 1987, Loubser spent 1989 in Australia studying rock art conservation under the joint auspices of the Getty Conservation Institute and Canberra University. In Australia he met various Aborigines and learned about their concerns with the "Dreamtime" places of their ancestors. Since the end of 1993, he has worked in the United States as an archaeologist/

rock art specialist at New South Associates, Inc., a cultural resource management firm located in Stone Mountain, Georgia. From his base at New South, and with the support and encouragement of his boss, Joe Joseph, he has traveled widely in the United States and met with various Native American groups, learning along the way what they think of their traditional cultural properties. He is author of *The Ethnoarchaeology of Venda-Speakers in Southern Africa* (Bloemfontein National Museum, 1991), *Ndebele Archaeology of the Pietersburg Area* (Bloemfontein National Museum, 1994), and the chapter on site conservation in the *Handbook of Rock Art Research* (AltaMira 2000), among other writings.

Made in the USA
Lexington, KY
24 January 2012